The Bristle Merchant's Daughter

by

John Salinsky

Foreword by Valerie Sanders
Professor of English Literature, University of Hull

authorHOUSE®

AuthorHouse™ UK Ltd.
500 Avebury Boulevard
Central Milton Keynes, MK9 2BE
www.authorhouse.co.uk
Phone: 08001974150

First published by AuthorHouse   9/23/2010

ISBN: 978-1-4520-3024-1 (sc)

This book is printed on acid-free paper.

Acknowledgments

I wish to thank my brother Kenneth Sanders for letting me read his own memoir of his childhood and also the transcript of a conversation with Florrie in which she talked about her early life.

Special thanks are also due to Alistair Stead who read every chapter, gave much valuable advice and encouragement and corrected my erratic punctuation. I had many helpful discussions with my wife Mary who also assisted in checking the manuscript. I am grateful to my niece, Professor Valerie Sanders, who gave me encouraging feedback and kindly wrote the foreword. I also thank Nick Bradley and Simon Oakeshott who were enthusiastic readers and reviewers of each chapter as it appeared. Thanks also to my cousins Philippa Travis, Peter Brostoff, Judith Caplan and Jonathan Rosenhead for their advice and permission to write about their parents and grandparents. Jonathan kindly gave me a copy of his grandmother's memoir.

Contents

Foreword

Valerie Sanders

'What do you remember about Grandma?' I asked my brother recently. 'The farm,' was his instant reply, which was just what I'd have said. Not a real farm, I must add, before you get the wrong idea of our grandmother as a bucolic matriarch, pumping milk from cows, and scattering seed among pecking fowl. It was a toy farm, kept under the spare bed, after many years of service in the family, and its livestock included two polar bears, a bison, and a chaise longue (which even at five I knew wasn't an animal). In those innocent days before IPods and Facebook we grandchildren liked nothing better than to play on the floor with the remnants of our parents' toy box, half-listening to the adult talk around us, which was usually of illness and business, and who had married whom. At meals I sat opposite the bookcase where my eyes were always level with two mysterious titles: *Totem and Taboo*, and *Moses and Monotheism*. Only years later did I realize that my grandmother must somehow along the way have read Freud, or at least acquired some of his books, along with Sir James Frazer's *Golden Bough*, and a handsomely embossed set of Dickens. The other object I associated her with was 'the Ewbank,' the faithful carpet-sweeper which was wheeled out after every meal to eradicate the crumbs. Grandma was indeed house-proud, the ritual folding of sheets and tablecloths a kind of stately country-dance as we pinched the corners together and walked towards each other until a sheet the size of a sail was reduced to a flat tablet ready for the airing cupboard. The ancient mangle in the garage testified to other, more vigorous laundering rituals.

Objects alone tell us only so much about a person's life. As children we understand very little of our grandparents', or even our parents' inner experiences. We think of them as there to serve us, until such time as we suddenly need to serve them. Florrie, the heroine of this semi-fictionalised biography, was a mother of three and grandmother of nine. Her life spanned almost the whole of the twentieth century

— from 1902 to 1999 — and she was of the first generation of her family to be born in England of Eastern European Jewish immigrants. A new century found them in a new country: a big northern city, not a fortress town or Polish village. As they learned the language and the customs of the place, her parents tried to fit in. The milkman vouched for her father's respectability, and the Foreign Office awarded them permanent citizenship. Their bright only daughter got to grammar school and then university; she wanted to be a doctor — but that proved too difficult. She married and became a mother, but we sensed that she always wanted something more. She was trapped by gentility, or perhaps timidity: fear of what the neighbours might say. She was not unconventional enough to take risks, but from time to time she collapsed, and the household briefly reconfigured itself. The three sons went to medical school and redeemed her missed opportunities, while their mother stayed at home and played Bridge with clever single women.

Florrie's tale is both the story of every woman of her generation — born a year after Queen Victoria's death, and dying in the Blair years of New Labour — and the story uniquely of herself. Some names have been changed, but not Florrie's. She deserves to keep that part of her identity intact, as she emerges, through the eyes of her youngest son John, for the first time, with a life and history of her own. I found it both moving and revelatory, and hope that it will be enjoyed just as much by a wider readership who never knew her, but perhaps knew someone like her, who started out in hope, but never quite achieved what she wished for.

Valerie Sanders, April 2010

Chapter 1:
Who were you before I was born?

I want to know more about my mother. Of course, I knew her very well when I was a child and in my teens. My father too. After that, our contact was more intermittent as I tried to make a go of being an adult: earning a living, getting married, raising a family, accumulating useless possessions that I couldn't throw out, relating to all sorts of people. Towards the end of her life, I drew closer to my mother again and I think I recaptured something of the relationship we had when I was little. Now I'm getting old myself. I am 68, both my parents are dead and my eldest brother has lost his memory. Everyone I used to know is getting old and everyone I work with is so much younger than I am. I am old enough to know, not just in theory, but in my bones, that I haven't all that much longer to go.

One thing I've noticed about people who are really near to death, is the way they want to talk to their parents again. Not the old folks, whom they used to visit dutifully in the old house or the old people's home, but the young parents, full of life and energy and colour. The beautiful mother. The strong, confident father. My mother sometimes asked me, when she was 90 and I visited her in the nursing home, have you seen Mother and Dad lately? At first I thought she meant my father (dead 20 years) and herself. Then I realised she was talking about her own parents, 40 years dead. She told me they had called to see her not long ago. Sat there on the bed just like you are doing. And were they still living in the same house? At the end of her life, she needed to talk to them and so she conjured them up to sit on her bed. Who else knows about this? Novelists, of course, and filmmakers. Kazuo Ishiguro has

3

written a whole book (*When We Were Orphans*) about a search for his young parents. Philip Roth's aging *Everyman* visits his parents in the cemetery and tells them: 'Your boy is seventy-one.' 'In the days that followed he had only to yearn for them to conjure them up, and not merely the bone parents of old age but the flesh parents of the boy still in bud…' In Ingmar Bergman's wonderful film *Wild Strawberries* the last scene shows the elderly Professor Borg having a dreamlike vision of his parents sitting side by side fishing. They wave to him cheerfully and he closes his eyes in tranquillity. They are still there for him.

I haven't yet reached the stage where my parents will appear spontaneously and sit on my bed for a chat. But I want to get to know them better. Especially my mother, but my father too. He will understand and won't mind taking second place. In any case her story is his story too. It's frustrating that I only knew her for less than half of her life. She was a remarkable woman. She could have done things if she'd had the opportunity. She was beautiful. She was talented. On good days, she could be suffused with gaiety. Her name was Fraydel, which means Joy, but she was known as Florrie. On bad days she was wracked with misery, driven by compulsions, stony in her depression. This much I know. But I need to be able to see her as a child in her parents' home, looking after her little brothers; a young woman getting aroused by thoughts of love and sex and intellectual talk and books and music; suffering from that terrible inner conflict that made her life such a struggle and that I wasn't supposed to know about. I want to explore that part of her life before I was born, that I didn't share. And then, after getting myself born about half way through, I shall re-examine and reflect on my relationship with her as I grew up and she grew old.

When I was quite a small child she wanted me to know about how I began. On my seventh birthday she gave me a book called *How You Began: A Child's Introduction to Biology* by Amabel Williams-Ellis. It described the process of the evolution of species, paralleled by the ontogeny of the human being from egg to adult. Because this was 1948, there was nothing whatever about how you were begat, but it was a marvellous book for its time and I have it still. Now I want to know how my mother began. I am not starting completely from nothing or even a tiny speck of jelly. I have a few facts to play with: a flimsy framework of information and anecdotes about her parents, her childhood, her education, how she met my father and so on. There are family stories, little scenes that illuminate her briefly at certain moments in her life that she would tell us about. But I need more. I need to be there, if only as a voyeur. Woody Allen (paying homage to Bergman) has episodes in his films when he becomes a privileged visitor to scenes from his own childhood, his young vigorous parents presiding. Using the idea of cinema I want to go further and visit, in my imagination, scenes from before I was born. Indeed, I mean to start even earlier by looking at the early life of my mother's parents who were born in another country in the previous century. This is what I shall do. I shall take a seat in my cinema of the mind and let my thoughts wander. I shall drift in and out of dreamlike states. After a while, if conditions are right, and I am not interrupted, the projector will whirr into action and the screen will light up. The first film we see is silent and in black and white and it flickers a little. Later on we shall have sound and colour. But this one is from the archives, carefully restored. It tells the story of my mother's parents and how they met.

Chapter 2:
Jacob and Rachel

We are in the little town of K somewhere in Eastern Europe, in the empire of the Czar. The year is 1895 or thereabouts. The street is lined with wooden houses mostly of one storey with steeply pitched roofs. The road is clotted with mud and full of horse-drawn vehicles. Wrinkled old men sit on the pavements, smoking and talking. As we move down the street, the houses get taller and I can see a cluster of simple shops. One has masses of second-hand clothes hung up in no particular order. There's a baker and a greengrocer and a fishmonger. One shop has large barrels on the pavement into which shoppers are plunging their hands. It's very noisy: shrieks, yells, laughter; but I can't make out what they are saying. There are noises of hammering and sawing. Horses stamping and whinnying. Now I can smell fish and vinegar, leather, sweat, spice. The pleasant smell of fresh bread wafts through the air. (This is odd, because you can't normally smell things at the cinema. Not from the screen anyway.) The men all wear hats or caps and long woollen coats. There are muscular men with enormous beards manhandling crates and barrels. Picking their way carefully are a few men in smart black coats and felt hats with brim and crown. There are women wearing long checked shawls, with children of all ages tumbling around them, laughing, crying, shouting.

Let us zoom in on this young man here. He is a good-looking fellow of about 20 with brown hair and a thick moustache but no beard. He is well dressed in a respectable suit and overcoat. He strides along in a confident way. Let me introduce you to Jacob my maternal grandfather, my mother's father. Jake is a young man who is going places. He is shortly going to leave this ramshackle town and become a successful businessman in another country. That will need all the self-confidence he can muster. But right now he is feeling in need of refreshment. He turns into the door of an old tavern. He doesn't know it yet but he is also on the brink of a romantic encounter. Before we follow him in I am going to freeze the frame and tell you a bit about how he came to be in the town of K. On second thoughts, I shall let you go on seeing pictures so it will be more a flashback than a freeze-frame with voice over.

Jacob was born in another little town called G about 10 miles to the west. His parents belonged to a community with a rich culture which was different from that of the rest of the population. In the many small towns and large villages like K and G, our people (as I shall call them) were actually the majority, but this did not make them feel secure. The two communities lived side by side but were not close. Their houses were usually separated by a boundary, maybe a river or a street or perhaps just an invisible line. Our people were tradesmen, artisans and shopkeepers. The others were largely peasant farmers. They would trade with us and exchange civilities when they were sober. But really they saw us as weird foreigners who had somehow occupied part of their land. We always seemed to have money when they were in need of it, which made them resentful. And their priests would sometimes hint in their sermons that we were ritual child-abusers. Although this was completely untrue and not widely believed, it added to our troubles. On the other hand, I have to say that the way our people kept to themselves with their distinctive dress and language did nothing to win them friends outside the community. Hostilities broke out from time to time, in which our people, being gentle and long-suffering, generally came off worst. But within their boundaries, surrounded by their family and friends, they could enjoy life for much of the time. Our complicated and demanding religion was an absorbing passion for many of the men. The women respected the importance of their devout and scholarly way of life and were in the main content to serve, feed and care for them. Naturally some of our young folk were discontented with what seemed to them a narrow and inward-looking way of life. They were aware of the intellectual discoveries of the century; the developments in science and literature and political economy. They could read about these things in books and magazines but that only made them more restless. They wanted to get out to the big cities where these forbidden fruits were available to be plucked and enjoyed. Some of their elders secretly sympathised. But on the whole they wanted our traditional way of life to continue and that meant that it mustn't be undermined by disruptive ideas from outside. Above all the children should marry each other and continue to practice the religion.

What was Jacob's position? He was a clever boy, but not an intellectual. He accepted our religion as a given and quite enjoyed the seasonal ceremonies. But he wasn't really convinced about the old man in the sky who was supposed to be in charge. Of course, he was too smart to tell anyone about these doubts. He was not a very spiritual young man. He could manage without poetry and philosophy and he certainly didn't want to study religious texts. But he did read the papers and he knew there was a larger world outside that was full of promise. His childhood had begun well but that happiness came to an end with the sudden death of his father from pneumonia at the age of 28 (no antibiotics in those days). Jacob was eight and his younger brother Isaac was only four. Their father had worked in the small brush factory which an enterprising citizen of G had started in the back yard of the bakery. In his teens Jake was employed by the brush factory although he also learned a bit of carpentry which would come in useful later on. You should remember that brushes – and especially the pigs' hair bristles that were bonded into their wooden handles – were of singular economic importance to my mother's family. This will seem strange at first. How can anyone make living out of hogs' bristles, let alone grow rich? Have patience. All this will be explained in due course. After a year or two, the boys' widowed mother set aside her grief and married a dapper little man called Josh with whom she had three more children.

The boys resented the intrusion into their mother's house and bed of a stranger who seemed loud mouthed and bossy, despite his small size. When more children arrived, Jacob and Isaac had to sleep in the warehouse. Their mother ran a grocery shop in G and had also developed a wholesale business for which she needed storage space. Seeing that relations between Jake and her new husband might boil over, she decided to send the boy to school in the small town of T where he could lodge with his maternal grandparents. Now Jacob's grandfather traded in those hog's bristles that I mentioned which were used to make brushes. He knew how buy them from local farmers and even how to order them from as far away as China, where the best quality hog bristles were – and are still – to be found. How did they get the pigs to part with their bristles? When I was a small child I was told that the animals liked to scratch themselves on posts which were specially provided by the farmers who then carefully collected any bristles that rubbed off. I can no longer believe this story which I think you will agree is the kind of thing adults make up to spare the feelings of a kind-hearted little boy who is fond of animals, even those deemed unfit to eat. It's much more likely, isn't it, that the pigs were killed for pork and sausages and every bristle they had was removed from their poor dead hides by boiling them. I still don't like to think of this too much. At any rate, the farmers provided the bristles and sold them to people like my great-great-grandfather. Having obtained an assortment of bristles, he would wash them, comb them and mix them to provide batches of different length and stiffness. These he would sell on to the local brush-makers of whom there were quite a few. What did they need all these brushes for? For painting, for sweeping, for cleaning their teeth. Well I can't be sure that they used toothbrushes, and it is possible that they still used bunches of twigs or indeed didn't brush them at all. But Grandfather's bristles were certainly used for toothbrushes in the next century until they were replaced by nylon. The coming of nylon was the beginning of the end for the bristle industry but by then it had served its purpose. I must now pick up the thread of my story.

In his adolescence, Jacob brooded like Hamlet. Unlike Hamlet he wanted to get away. His little brother Isaac had quietly disappeared when he was only 16 and was now doing well for himself in the clothing trade in England. In his occasional letters he urged Jacob to come and join him. But Jacob was a bit more cautious and besides he didn't like having his life organised by his kid brother. For him, it seemed enough to begin with to move to a different town.

In the town of K (where we were standing until I introduced this flashback) there lived one of Jacob's father's brothers, whose name was Mendel. Jacob got on well with his Uncle Mendel and his Aunt Sarah and the ever-increasing number of little cousins. He wrote a letter. He was invited to visit. The visit was prolonged. He became a member of his uncle's family. Mendel was a jobbing carpenter who also made furniture in a small way. He taught his willing nephew to become a better woodworker and Jacob enjoyed the work. But at the back of his mind he kept a big idea about the potential of bristles.

The scene dissolves smoothly back to K and we see Jacob opening the wooden door and entering the tavern. It is a shabby old place smelling of wine and stale food. There are only a few drinkers there and there is a low mutter of male conversation. This pub is an unprepossessing place where you wouldn't want to linger. But behind the counter is a striking-looking girl. She is about 20 with long reddish hair and light blue eyes. She greets the smart-looking young man with a smile and for a few seconds the two young people stand silently gazing at each other. Their mutual contemplation is interrupted by a shout from the back of the house. A thickset man comes up the cellar steps with a small barrel of wine, sets it down on the floor, gives an order to the girl and goes back down again. He calls her Rachel. She must be his daughter. Rachel laughs, showing nice white teeth, and says to Jake: so what would you like? Jake orders a glass of good quality wine and some pickled herring with bread. The father comes up with one more barrel, nods at the young man and then disappears into the back. There are no more customers, so the boy and girl can talk.

Now this Rachel is a rather special girl. She has been to a superior school in the city. She knows a thing or two about life outside the tight little world where our people huddle close together. She knows history and literature. She loves music and can play Mozart and Chopin on the piano. She can even play Liszt's *La Campanella*. Jake has to confess his ignorance of music, but Rachel doesn't mind that he can't share that part of her life. He has other qualities that attract her. He is brisk and determined. He knows what he wants. They agree that the town of K is a bit of a dump. Sure, the fairs and festivals and the weddings are fun, but after a while they are all much the same. Every so often a visitor from outside appears and tells anyone who will listen about the world outside. Theatres and concerts, sighs Rachel. Nice houses, opportunities, says Jacob. A man with a few ideas and the will to succeed could make a life. Bring up a family in comfort. Rachel blushes. She knows where this is going and she is pleased and excited but it had better not be too fast. A slight change of subject is required. And another thing, she says. It's so dangerous here. You never know when the Other People will get nasty and come in a gang to rob us and burn our houses, and she stopped and didn't mention the other things they could and did do before they got tired of it and went away. Then there was the Army, whose recruiting sergeants could descend suddenly on our people and take away the young men for a life of military service for a cause that was not theirs and from which they might never return to their families. Mostly people accepted everything that could happen with a shrug and a stoic fatalism. What can you do? they said. And, ironically, so long as we have our health. But Rachel and Jacob had nothing but contempt for this spineless attitude. There must be an alternative. Rachel pointed out that there were several alternatives, all involving going abroad. Some of the more nationalistic of our people were trying to set up a new state in the middle of a desert. Jacob didn't fancy that. Those people were too earnest. Then, continued Rachel, people were leaving all the time to go to America. Some came back for a visit after a few years, showed off their fine clothes and amazed their relatives with tales of life in the New World where even our people were as rich as the nobility over here. Others were never heard of again, it was true. There's my brother Isaac in England, said Jacob. Wonderful, said Rachel, he could help us. I suppose so said Jacob, doubtfully. The truth was he had no great wish to see his energetic, talkative, little brother again as they had never got on all that well. You can see that Rachel had to work on my grandfather, fanning the flickering flame of his pioneering spirit and trying to convince him to take her away. All this is important for what eventually happened but you want to know more about their courting and so do I. What happens next?

Well, Jacob becomes a regular visitor. The elders of our community in the town of K are quite liberal, and young men and women are allowed to go for walks in the town and even into the country so long as they go as a group. Of course there are times when one or two (usually two) people will linger in a shop or by the lake and get left behind for a while. In this way Jacob and Rachel continue their conversations. They have a furtive kiss by the lake. They hold hands as they run to catch up with the others and be home in time for tea. Naturally people talk. Rachel's father and Jacob's uncle speak together and agree that a marriage was to be encouraged, in fact the sooner the better.

And so they get married. I'm not going to describe the traditional wedding with the traditional costumes, with the tables groaning with food, and the old folks cackling, and the squeaky village band, and the vigorous dancing with the bride and groom held high in the air, and the tears and laughter and jokes because I can't really do that Fiddleron-the-Roof kind of stuff and there are plenty of other places you can read about it.

I would rather eavesdrop on one of Jake and Rachel's conversations a few days before the wedding and try to get inside their heads. We are down by the lake again and there is no one else around. They sit on an old bench, Jake with his arm around Rachel's waist. She lets her head rest fondly on his shoulder. Things have moved on! Jake is now taking the initiative as men like to do when it comes to practical matters such as buying tickets. Jake says we have to get to Hamburg. That's where all the ships sail from, taking people to England and America. There's a man there who can get us tickets for a steamer, I have his address. Shall we go to England or America? asks Rachel, snuggling close. Anything seems possible with Jacob by her side. He is big and strong. And there is courage in his moustache. America will cost a lot more, he says. But people say there are more opportunities. I have some money saved, she murmurs. I know, sweetheart. But my Uncle was telling me that we have some cousins in the North of England who will find us a home and get us started. And there's your brother, Rachel reminds him, stroking his hair. Yes, that's true. You know he wanted to go to America but he gave some of his money to a poor man he met on the dockside who had been robbed. Then he only had enough for a ticket to England. Now he's in England and he's doing well there, he says. So he can help us!

You shouldn't be too proud to learn from him, Jacob, just because he's younger than you. He will speak English fluently by now. We will have to learn English too, she goes on. I already know some from school. I will teach you what I know. Oh, Jacob, I want to live in a city where there are concerts and theatres! I want to see a real opera on the stage with an orchestra and costumes and lots of people. I want to learn about books and poetry; maybe I could become a teacher. But I will miss the family, she says, suddenly remembering that it's such a long way and they won't come back except perhaps for a short visit. She looks downcast for a few seconds, and then her face clears and she says but we'll have our own family, won't we Jacob? And you will start a business and we'll have a nice house and I'll cook the kind of food you like and we'll light candles and recite our prayers just as we always have done.

They are so innocent. To me they look like Charlie Chaplin and Paulette Goddard in *Modern Times* striding off down the road with touching optimism. They seem determined to go, don't they? We can only hope their luck holds and they realise those dreams. But what do their families think? I bet some of them disapprove. Here they are in Rachel's mother's kitchen with her parents. They have just finished eating. I don't want you to go, says here mother tearfully. I'll never see my little girl again. Father shakes his head. It will be very risky, he says. They may arrest you when you try to cross the border. And some of those boats are not safe. Even if you get to America (England, Papa) even if you get to England then, not everyone succeeds. We only hear of the few that do well. Some are starving maybe (her mother sobs in the background). Life is not so bad here (he stretches out his arms as if to enfold the children). And you are among your own people. The way of life will be different there. What will they give you to eat? asks her mother. It may not be suitable. We are willing to take all the risks, says Jake (and Rachel looks at him admiringly). We are young and strong and willing to work hard and things here will only get worse. Lots of people have gone already and there will be more. You'll be alone among strangers, no one to help you, wails the mother.

I'll write to you Mum, says Rachel. And we'll come back and visit. Seriously, Jacob, says her father, do you know anyone in England? Why yes, says Jacob. There's my little brother Isaac. He writes to me that he has his own business now. Imagine that! And there's a fellow called Joe Pushkar, who comes from G. He has a brush factory in a place called Lidz, not far from where the boat will dock. He will give me work there to get me started. And there's a whole community of our people already in the town, they help you get a place to live. The women will show Rachel where the markets are and that sort of thing. We will soon be Englanders! Englanders, chuckles the father, sucking on his pipe and his wife hugs her daughter tightly. Take care of my Rachel she pleads and Jacob says she will be safe with him and he's such a big strong confident boy you have to believe him.

Chapter 3 :
A new life in Lidz

So they went, one day, with their bags and their bundles. The horse-drawn cart came for them before sunrise. There were several other young people on it already and they stretched out willing arms to help our young couple aboard. Rachel brought a bundle of food for them, fish cakes and potatoes and half a loaf of bread and some sweet biscuits. It was a long journey of several hours along deserted roads and through sleeping villages but no one bothered them. When they got to the border, the driver showed the soldiers some documents with all their names on. There was some money too that they had all contributed. The soldier stuffed the money in to his greatcoat pocket, returned the documents and waved them through. Now they were in Germany heading for the port city of Hamburg. But wait a minute! Hamburg was hundreds of miles away. I am confabulating here because there are gaps in my story. Part of the footage has been lost, and I'm trying to cut what's left together but it's not convincing. Horse and cart indeed! They must have gone by train, maybe to Warsaw and then via Berlin to Hamburg? Let's just say that they got to the port one way or another, and they still had enough money for steerage tickets on one of the many modern steamers crossing the Baltic, the North Sea and the Atlantic. In steerage between the decks there were no proper cabins, but the young couple were given some space of their own with a canvas awning for a bit of privacy. They stood on deck, their arms round each other, watching the land recede. When it got dark they lay down together on the mattress they had brought with them and whispered together about what they would do in England. On the evening of the second day they reached the North Sea port of Hull and disembarked.

A guide was waiting to show them onto the train, and they sat side by side, clutching their bundles, watching the flat pastures of the Vale of York give way to the belching chimneys and huddled houses of the industrial West Riding of Yorkshire, until the train puffed its way into Leeds City Station. On the train they met one of those knowledgeable people who had arrived in Leeds several years before and was on his way back from some business or other in Hull. Got relatives have you? he enquires. They eagerly give names. Oh yes? I know them slightly. But don't you worry. All our people live in the same part of town and there's a system for sorting out the new arrivals and getting them to their families if we can find them. And, if we can't, we have guides who will show you a house where you can stay. Got a little money have you? They keep quiet. Got a trade then? Jacob offers his woodworking skills, and the man nods. Soon be on your feet I reckon. Mind you it's not luxury in the Leylands.

The Leylands! It sounds like lush country meadows but really it was a terrible slum. Rotten, decaying houses, huddled together round exposed courtyards, no proper sanitation, cold, damp, overcrowded. It was much worse than the little towns and villages they had left. But people were friendly and their bossiness was welcome when you were cold, hungry and homesick. A taciturn man asked them where they came from, pored over a list on a grubby piece of paper and ordered a boy to take them to a house where someone else from the town of K lived. Jacob asked about Isaac but the man didn't know him. Someone else said he was a big shot who didn't live in the Leylands no more. He had become an Englisher. Was this good news or bad? As they trudged along the mean streets they could see that every other house was a workshop. Men ran in and out with bales of cloth on their shoulders. Others pushed long trolleys hung with garments, shouting for people to get out of their way. Through the grimy windows Rachel could see men cutting cloth, men and women bent over sewing machines and others banging huge irons down on steaming blue and grey suits. In some houses the front room had become a food shop open to the street. The smells of herring and newly baked bread were fleeting but comforting as they passed by. Finally, they arrived at their new home, a little attic room with an old double bed, a table and two chairs. Share of a kitchen.

Jacob fought down the feeling of being trapped and wishing he was back at Uncle Mendel's. Rachel was already talking to the woman from the next-door room. And she was thinking: when Jacob finds work we'll move out of here. And he did find work. There was a furniture maker who needed an additional assistant and Jacob was skilled enough to be taken on. They made a little home together in the Leylands, and were happy despite the noise and the squalor because Jacob had a job, and they had food to eat, and the neighbours were their own kind and friendly. And most of all because they had each other in their rusty old iron sprung bed at night where they could lie with their arms round each other and make love.

I'm going to leave them there now, with an old-fashioned iris wipe. That's probably not the correct cinematic term but it's the one where a circular frame appears round the picture and closes in like a camera iris until the scene is gone. Because the next significant event is the meeting with brother Isaac. When we iris out again, the year is 1900, Jacob and Rachel are 23 and 22 respectively and Isaac whom we are about to meet is just 19! A 19-year-old big shot who has already moved out of the immigrant quarter and become a proper Englander. He arrives one day, picking his way carefully over the mud and rubbish and worse that decorates the Leyland streets until he finds the house where he has been told his brother and new sister-in-law are living. Isaac is slimmer and taller than Jacob and has wavy fair hair and glasses. He doesn't yet have the diabetes that will alter the course of his life, but not curtail it. He knocks on the door and Jacob opens it. The brothers greet each other warmly and embrace cautiously. Jacob introduces Rachel who notices Isaac's neatly cut suit and smart slightly muddied shoes. Isaac notices that Rachel is attractive. He too has a young wife whom we will meet when we get our invitation. Isaac accepts a seat and asks Jacob for news of the family. This keeps them going in an animated way for half an hour. Rachel makes tea (lemon and lumps of sugar) and listens carefully. When they talk about work she learns that Isaac now has his own little tailoring business employing men and women in the Leylands to make up suits for him to sell to the customers who come to his shop.

He has done well, thinks Rachel Can he help Jacob to advance himself, she asks boldly. Jacob knows all about bristles. I hear there's a brush-maker here in the Leylands, says Jacob thinking, why do I have to ask our kid for favours? Yes, yes, says Isaac impatiently, but you don't

The Bristle Merchant's Daughter

want to work for him. You can do better than that. This confident, bright-eyed boy seems to know everything. And Jacob thinks, he's such a wise-guy. I wonder if he still wets his bed. Come to the house says Isaac grandly. Come and meet Annie my wife. She also comes from K, Rachel. She knows your family. Here's the address. It's not far. Anyone will show you. Come for dinner on Friday night and we'll talk business.

Friday nights are special for our people. The Sabbath is welcomed in at sunset with candles and a little prayer, recited by my Great Auntie Annie with her fingers bunched over her eyes. Then the four young people sit down at the neatly laid table with its spotless white cloth, gleaming glassware and silver-plated cutlery. Isaac is relaxed and expansive in his nice stone-built house in Brunswick Street. Annie serves them chopped liver and onions followed by fried fish. It's just like being at home with Mum and Dad in K, thinks Rachel, with a pang of regret. Isaac tells them how he started the business and how it's still expanding. He already has his eye on a better house, round the corner in Brunswick Place which has iron gates at end, no traffic and trees lining the street on one side. After supper the men say grace, which you are supposed to do, and then start talking about money (which you are not). Isaac's advice is that Jacob should make use of his knowledge of the bristle trade and his contacts abroad. You may not know it, he says, but there are lots of brush-makers round here. Why is that, asks Rachel who is always curious. Isaac explains that they make paintbrushes, sweeping brushes and even fine brushes for artists. But the most important customers are the cotton-mill owners across the Pennine Hills in Lancashire. It seems that cotton fibres produce clouds of dust (which make the workers cough) and they go through hundreds of brushes, sweeping it all away. Now, says Isaac, turning back to Jacob, if you could rent some premises, you could import the bristles, get some men to help you clean them or whatever you do, pack them up and then sell them on to the brush-makers. Rent a building, says Jacob doubtfully, where am I going to get that sort of money? Then Isaac produces his masterstroke. You and I will go into partnership! He says. I will provide the capital (I have some put by in the Building Society) and you will provide the expert knowledge. Jacob hesitates and his eye movements suggest an intense inner processing of this information and its implications. Time stands still for a moment. Then Rachel takes his hand and looks up into his eyes and says to Isaac, that's a wonderful idea and so thoughtful of you, so generous! And Annie beams at them and at her clever husband who thinks of everything and everyone. And Rachel thinks to herself, we'll need a contract drawn up by a lawyer because I don't completely trust his brother, but this is the way to go! Then, one day, we will have a house like this, in Brunswick Place with the trees, even. Meanwhile, says Annie, you must move in with us, there's plenty of room and I don't like to think of you living in those terrible Leylands.

And so a deed of partnership was drawn up. Equal shares of the profits for the two brothers. An old warehouse was rented and subsequently purchased in a run down street not far away. Jacob knew that imported bristles were sold by auction in London, a long journey of 200 miles, but they needed to go. Isaac of course had been to London several times. They set off on that first visit to the capital, not from the City station where the trains brought in the immigrants from Hull, but from the smaller Central station down the road. Through here pass the trains run by a different company between London and Scotland. These trains have huge, black steam engines whose funnels belch greasy smoke and hissing clouds of sooty water vapour. They are very long. They even have dining cars. Years later, a specially smart train called The Yorkshire Pullman ran from Leeds to London and I shall always remember with pleasure going with my parents on one of these on my first visit to London in 1951. We sat in luxurious armchairs with tables in front of us. When it got dark, the curtains were drawn and pale pink lamps came on. And cheerful uniformed stewards came and served us lunch without our having to move. But I don't think in 1901 they had Pullmans yet. And Isaac and Jacob brought their own lunches, wrapped up for them by their loving little wives so that, away from home, they would not be tempted to eat the wrong sort of food. The train rattled and hissed and whistled its way down to London and spilt them out among its teeming multitudes (if my language gets a little more grandiose and poetical, you should put it down to the excitement of describing my grandfather's first sight of the metropolis which I now take so much for granted). They walk from the Kings Cross Station down to the City and the East End (lots more of our people) and they find, at last, the auction rooms. My grandfather has never taken part in a bristle auction or indeed an auction of any kind. They go into the showroom with lots of other people. How astonishing that there should be so many bristle merchants in one town; but this is London, as Isaac points out.

In the showroom, the brothers browse over bristles. It's just a lot of hair to Isaac but Jacob looks up their provenance and feels them between his fingers as he was taught to do by his grandfather. Then a bell rings and it is time for the auction. The large room is crowded with buyers, mostly Englishers, but some with the look of Our People. On a platform at the front, the auctioneer mutters and drones incomprehensibly. Jacob can't make out what's going on. He's told Isaac the lots he wants but Isaac hasn't said a word. He whispers: I think that was the five and a quarter inch Shanghai I wanted. What happened? Isaac, his gaze fixed on the auctioneer says, don't worry, I bought it. He tells Jacob it's all done by discreet nods and hand signals. Soon he gets the idea and buys a couple of cases of six and a half inch bristles from Tientsin. All the best bristles come from China. I know this because 60 years later I had a student vacation job at Rostov bristles. My three uncles (sons of Jacob and Rachel) paid me half a crown an hour and I got three large mugs of tea a day. The bristles came in large packing cases each containing 100 wedge shaped packets of bristles labelled 'China National Animal By-product Corporation', plus the name of the province they came from: Hankow, Tientsin, Shanghai or Chungking. Each packet weighed one Chinese catty and a Chinese catty was equal to exactly one and third pounds. How this equivalence was agreed in the darkest days of the British Empire's relationship with China I have no idea, but it is the kind of useless information you never forget.

So Jacob and Isaac buy lots of catties of best Chinese hog bristles and arrange for them to be conveyed to the warehouse in Leeds. Then they have dinner in an East End restaurant which provided the kind of food our people are supposed to eat. They were well satisfied with their day's work. Jacob was already planning a schedule of visits to the brush makers in the West Riding of Yorkshire with samples of his newly acquired stock. Should he get a horse and cart? He knew how to drive a horse from his days in G so that was no problem. Or should he go by train? Or even get one the new motor cars that were beginning to be seen about the city.

We'll fade out on Jacob's thoughts about means of transportation and fade in a few months later to find a thriving little business in which Jacob and Isaac are partners. They have a rented warehouse with plenty of room for their collection of packing cases filled with Chinese bristles. They have workbenches where the bristles can have a mix and match and a trim. They have employees in the shape of two middle-aged men from the old country who have worked with bristles. One is mild and easy going; the other is prickly and raises awkward questions about their conditions of employment. Isaac says he is a communist. They have an office with a Dickensian high desk and stool where Isaac shows Jacob how to keep the accounts in leather bound ledger, in black ink with a scratchy steel pen. Twice a day, a horse drawn wagon stops outside the front door and is loaded with cases of Rostov bristles for the brush makers of Leeds and several surrounding towns. Money starts to come in. Back at home, Rachel is getting restless for a place of her own. Soon there is enough money to rent a house in Cromwell Street. It's not Brunswick Place and it's still the Leylands but it's a lot better than the old place and it's theirs.

What has Rachel been doing while the brothers were setting up the business? She has been exploring the Victorian English city and found out what it has to offer. Her most gratifying discovery is music! There are concerts every fortnight in the Town Hall where she can hear an orchestra for a few pence, sitting up in the gallery. This was only rarely possible in the old country and involved perilous trips to Białystok or even Warsaw.

Leeds had the Grand Theatre and Opera House which, twice a year, was true to the second half of its name and had a visit from The Carl Rosa Opera, a touring company run by a European émigré. Here she could see and hear wonderful performances of *Traviata, Rigoletto* and *Figaro.* She would walk home, wrapped in her shawl, unafraid of the possible dangers of the urban street at night, singing to herself, trying to make the experience last till she could get home and tell Jacob all about it. When they moved into their new house, in a terrace in Evelyn Street, she persuaded Jacob that they need a piano, and with the first profits of the business a second-hand upright was lugged into the front parlour by two sweating deliverymen. Rachel found a man to tune it and was soon practising every day, using the music she had been careful to bring with her. She was pleased with their progress. Jacob had proved to be a good husband (even if he was cool about opera) and a good provider. Their new house was spacious and their own, even if the neighbouring Englishers were a little rough and noisy at the weekends and not all that friendly. Still, Elsie, the woman next door, had become a good friend even though she was not from the old country. Elsie was about Rachel's age and already had two little children who were very sweet and appealing. I think you can see where I'm heading. Did people make decisions to have children in those days? The only effective contraception was abstinence so I don't think so. Perhaps she was already pregnant when she looked at Elsie and her baby smiling at each other. Perhaps she had already felt the first stirrings of My Mother inside her.

Soon it will be time for Florrie to make her entrance.

Chapter 4:
Birth, childhood and adolescence

January 20th 1902. Last year Queen Victoria died. Today my mother will be born in an old saggy double bed in a not very nice terrace house in a not quite slum area of the City of L. Rachel has felt some sporadic pains for several days now but suddenly they come on more sharply and last for longer. Jacob is out at work, but her friend Elsie James next door will go for the midwife who lives not far away. When the pain gives her a respite, she puts on her coat and hat and hurries next door to knock up Mrs James. Elsie puts on her coat and says she will run for Mrs Briggs. So Rachel who can feel another pain coming on goes home to wait. Jacob will be home for his tea soon so she thinks about doing some cooking but another pain, stronger than before, makes her sigh and sit down instead.

Fanny Briggs, the midwife, has seen it all before and is reassuring. These new people are a bit strange, and not everyone likes them with their funny accents that you can hardly understand. But the women are made just the same as we are, even if they do get a bit hysterical in labour. And they are very grateful for her services. She finds the stove and puts on some water to boil; assembles as many towels and cloths as she can; makes Rachel undress for bed and examines her. The head is down now, she notes with satisfaction. Should be fine if she doesn't bleed or get a fever. Rachel smiles nervously at her helper who offers her a cup of tea. I ought to get my husband his tea, she says. Don't worry about him, retorts Briggs. He'll be so pleased with the baby he'll go and have a few drinks with his mates instead. Except being one of the Newcomers he probably won't. They don't go to the pubs much, which is in their favour. Except it means they don't get to know any one but each other. Keep to themselves. Have their own special churches and so on. Well, live and let live. Another contraction. Rachel submits to an examination from Mrs Briggs's professional hands. Dilating nicely. Soon be time to push, she tells her patient. Rachel nods and smiles. Inside she is afraid but also filled with a dream-like wonder.

An hour later, labour is progressing. Then there are footsteps and the front door creaks open. A male voice says something in a foreign tongue which must mean 'I'm home!' Mrs Briggs runs down the stairs with her finger to her lips and hisses: Shush Mister, your wife is in labour and I am attending to her. She is doing well. But this is women's business. Sit yourself down here and I'll tell you when you have a child. Not long now. The husband is a strong good-looking young fellow with a moustache but no beard and no ringlets. He has a goodish suit, not one of those long coats that some of them wear.

She is pleased that he seems to accept her authority and her competence. He's not getting agitated or wanting a doctor sent for, like some of them will. Of course a doctor is sometimes needed and Mrs Briggs knows who to send for if it comes to it. If he's around today that is, but we'll worry about that if it happens. A cry from Rachel sends her hurrying back and it's time to push! I won't do the whole stage two of labour because you've heard it before and seen it on the screen in all its gory glory.

The blood smeared hair, the crumpled little face emerging etc etc. Let's cut to the point where rapt Rachel receives the wrapped little bundle in her arms and smiles with delight at the sight of her blue-eyed little girl. Now Jacob is allowed in too and he grins with happiness and relief. Of course he needs a son to help with the business in due course but a little daughter will be fine to start with. They agreed to call her Freydel with Florrie as her English name. Where they got Florrie from I don't know. There was a popular music hall artist called Florrie Ford, and Florrie was one of a number of now outdated Edwardian names for girls. Florrie would rather have been called 'Florence', a name that would have fitted her good looks and her dignity. I love visiting Florence because it is such a beautiful city and the cradle of the Renaissance. I also think of it as my mother's city, although sadly she never had a chance to see it.

Florrie was to be an only child for just two years. Then, at regular two-year intervals, three little brothers popped out of Rachel's womb, each coming more easily than the last. What were they like? Harry, the eldest, was strong, active and adventurous from the start. He would grow up to ride a motorbike, to get in to fights (and win most of them), to be very attractive to women, to get what he wanted except for one thing that none of them had, and we'll talk about it later. So that's Harry, a good strong elder brother and role model. Next to appear, two years later, was Abe who was a quieter child and made Rachel weep for him because he was lame. His poor little left leg was clearly not right from the start. It was shorter than the other one, bent slightly outwards and wouldn't support him properly when he tried to walk. They saw a doctor who said he could have a surgical boot to equalise the length but there was nothing else to be done and he would probably never walk. He had congenital dislocation, or dysplasia of the hip which was known about but not regarded as treatable. Rachel agonised over what she had done wrong to inflict such damage on a baby in her womb. She asked Jacob, who told her it wasn't her fault although he too wondered secretly if it was some sort of curse or retribution from the almighty. You will be pleased to hear that in the end he did walk but suffered pain all his life which he put up with stoically because he was able to find pleasures in life to compensate him, principally music, wine and the love of a woman who didn't mind that he was lame. The youngest brother, Hyman, was perfectly sound and healthy. He was always called 'Benny', a nickname he acquired at school. He grew up to be interested in photography and music, had good social skills and served as an officer in the second war. They were three very bright boys who could have done anything they wanted intellectually. But their ambitions were to be frustrated by their father and by Rostov Bristles.

When Florrie was only three years old and had one little brother, she started at Cross Stamford Street Junior Mixed and Infants School. Here the boys and girls sat in pairs at long dark brown desks and were taught their letters and numbers. On the first day, their teacher welcomed then by throwing handfuls of sweets into the air and encouraging the children to catch them. Like most of the other girls, Florrie wore a white pinafore over her long dress. Her long light brown wavy hair was parted on the right and she wore a ribbon tied in a bow on the left. There were about 40 children in the class. The room was heated only by an iron stove and was often cold in winter, especially if the coal ran out. Although school was basic compared with our own day, it was well organised and monitored by school Visitors who appeared regularly to make sure that the teaching standard was maintained and the attendance recorded properly. There was a nurse who checked everyone's hair for lice and their scalp for ringworm. If any infestation was discovered the nurse would order the child to go home and not come back until they were clear. There were also outbreaks of measles, chickenpox and whooping cough for which the school had to be closed, by order of the visiting doctor. Sometimes there was no school for a month. One little boy was taken to hospital wrapped in a blanket and was never seen again.

But on the whole they were happy and healthy. Florrie was, of course, a bright little girl, eager to learn and was soon able to read and write. There were also regular lessons in singing, dancing and drawing. Later on she would learn sewing and knitting.

The school was only 200 yards away from home, so by the time she was five she was able to walk there by herself and come home for her dinner. She would have porridge and a glass of milk for breakfast while her mother fed the baby, and Brother Harry sat in his high chair eating a piece of black bread and chattering away. Already she was helping Rachel to look after the little ones. Rachel had decided that as Florrie was the eldest and a girl it was right for her to be trained in this role as soon as possible. So, a year after Rachel has had her fourth and last baby, Florrie is already giving the two boys their tea and changing the baby's nappy. By the age of seven, she is beginning to feel some resentment about having all this responsibility. The older boys are lively and cheeky and not always easy to keep in order when Rachel is out shopping or visiting. Harry is very popular with the neighbours. He keeps disappearing and Florrie has to run up and down the street looking for him.

When Florrie was seven years old a number of significant changes happened in the family. First of all she moved from the Infants to the Girls School next door, where her abilities were soon recognised by her new teachers. Second, Jacob and Rachel were at last able to move out of the Leylands. Our people were generally getting more prosperous and were heading north up the Chapeltown Road. Jacob found a small but nice house to rent in Evelyn Street where they had a bit of garden for the children to play. In their new house the lights were electric instead of gas. Jacob showed Florrie the big brass switch in the parlour with its round ribbed base and taught her how to press hard until it clicked down and the whole room was flooded with light.

The neighbours were better than in the Leylands and less likely to come home drunk when the pubs shut and beat up their wives. Florrie still had the occasional nightmare about a struggle on the doorstep of the house opposite and the sight of a crying woman with blood on her face. Evelyn Street was more respectable.

The third change was in Jacob's business partnership. He and Isaac had been increasingly unhappy with each other. Isaac resented having to spend time helping his elder brother when he had two businesses of his own which needed attention. Jacob felt that Isaac spent too little time at Rostov Bristles considering he was taking home fifty per cent of the profits. The brothers quarrelled. Florrie overheard them shouting at each other in the lounge at Evelyn Street and was afraid there would soon be blood on their faces. But it didn't come to that. They argued loudly and then quietly agreed to separate. The partnership was dissolved. Isaac withdrew his capital and Jacob was able to borrow some more from Rachel's cousin who was a well-established baker.

Would he be able to manage on his own, asked Rachel. Jacob looked at his three little sons and said, soon they will be my partners: J. Rostov and Sons, Bristle Merchants. The business would grow and be able to provide for their families too. And what about Florrie? They agreed that Florrie would get married and her husband would take care of her.

Meanwhile Florrie was expected from an early age to do a share of the housework, which was laborious in those days. I'll just give you a brief idea of what had to be done. In the morning the ashes had to be scraped out of the grate and a new fire laid in the kitchen and living room. Coal had to be brought in from the coal place outside the back door. Floors had to be scrubbed with hard soap smelling of disinfectant. The wooden table had to be scrubbed. Beds had to be made. The whole house was swept and dusted every day. This was possibly due to an obsessional streak in Rachel that we haven't noticed before. Unhappily as it turned out, she passed this tendency on to Florrie, possibly through her genes and certainly by example and training. In Florrie it was to become a dominant preoccupation and, at times, an illness.

To continue the list of domestic duties, the family washing, including terry cloth nappies, had to be done by hand with the aid of a 'copper' boiler and a corrugated washboard. And cutlery made of silver plate, mostly wedding presents from old Europe, had to be vigorously polished once a week. Boots had to be polished, socks and stockings darned and buttons sewed on. More enjoyably, Rachel taught little Florrie to cook. She showed her all the traditional homeland ways with fish and fowls and also some good local dishes including Yorkshire Pudding and Apple Pie. There were no convenience foods and all the vegetables had to be washed and peeled. Did the boys learn to cook? I don't suppose so, do you? Did they help with the housework? When they were older they had to make their own beds and dry the crockery after Rachel or Florrie had washed it. Occasionally their father took a turn at washing up plates and cutlery but he drew the line at encrusted cooking pots and pans which he described as 'nasties'.

Now I think it's time for me to try and enter into the head of my heroine. Up to now you may have noticed that my narrative has been slightly distanced. I have compared it to watching an old black and while silent film; it affords a view into a distant past but it's hard to get close to the characters and share their feelings. Now I want to experience Florrie as she experienced herself. Not just up close and personal but from the inside. To feel what she felt, to vibrate in sympathy with her vocal cords as she speaks. To hear her heart beat and ride the waves of her emotions. You may ask how this is to be done considering I am a person of the opposite gender and that I never knew her in the first 39 years of her life. I think I can do it because, as her child, *I have already been inside her.* For 40 weeks I was part of her as she breathed, walked, talked, laughed cried, ate, digested, excreted and did everything else. I was aware of her. And she was aware of me. She felt my movements in her womb and we communed with each other. Later on during my nine months of breast feeding, we shared that 'maternal reverie' in which unspoken thoughts of love would be exchanged with soft glances, cooing sounds and the contact of our bodies, hers feminine, maternal, smelling of woman; mine deliciously baby-smooth, smelling of infant freshness, milk and poo.

Did she love her parents? Of course she did. Rachel was affectionate but she could also be strict. With the arrival of successive little brothers she became a little harassed and as we have seen, she addressed the problem by appointing Florrie as first assistant and little deputy mother. Florrie was passionately fond of her father as little girls are. At this age she loved to sit on his brown-trousered knee and play with his watch and chain. When he hugged her she felt safe and when she kissed his cheek she felt the bristles which seemed related to the bristles at work that sustained the whole family. At school, she was lively and affectionate and made friends easily. At the junior school (girls only) she enjoyed the lessons and felt the warmth of the teachers' appreciation. My mum was a bright, clever little girl with blue eyes, wavy brown hair and a lovely, serene smile. Only the responsibility for her brothers weighed on her mind. She loved them as individuals and felt especially tender towards little Abe with his limp and his surgical boot. But as a group they could tease and mock her. She would put them to bed when her parents were out at friends and they would refuse to stay there, dancing round in their nightshirts, giggling, shouting and demanding snacks. And with their friends, they were even worse to her because, as they pointed out, she was a girl. Although Florrie was the eldest, Harry seemed to be her parents' favourite. Her father would talk proudly about his three sons and sometimes she would feel that at home a girl was just a servant and a nursemaid, whereas at school she was a prized pupil, destined for academic success.

Still, as the eldest she had some importance. When she was eight her mother started her on the piano. She had to go to the house of a whiskery old gentleman who taught her scales and arpeggios and also allowed her to play some simple tunes. When he was demonstrating a scale she would gaze at his profile, fascinated by the way she could see his cheek through his transparent fair side-whiskers. At home, she was reluctant to practice especially in winter. The piano was in the front parlour, otherwise used only for entertaining on special occasions. There was no fire and the cold made her hands feel numb. When she tried to rebel, Rachel quietly made a hot water bottle and sat patiently beside her while she practised. When her hands were too cold she would rest them on the bottle on her mother's lap and then play some more. It was really Rachel's company she liked.

We know that Rachel needed music to nourish her, and she wanted her children to have music in their lives as well. When they were old enough Abe learned the piano with the pale whiskered gentleman too, and Benny learned the violin. Only Harry resisted a musical training and was allowed to have his way. Rachel still wanted to go to operas and concerts and would sometimes take Florrie with her. It was exciting to go out on her own with mother while the others stayed at home.

28

The Grand Theatre lived up to its name. They would nudge their way through a crowd of people in the foyer, Florrie hanging on to Rachel's hand. Then up the great staircase to dress circle level and finally up some narrower stairs without carpets to the gallery.

She loved listening to the overture and waiting for the moment when the big red curtain would go up. She loved the singing characters and was entranced by the music. When the heroine became ill, Florrie's eyes stung with hot tears, and when the heroine died (as she nearly always did) she was saddened and puzzled. Why did the girl always die? She demanded of her mother. It wasn't fair. But Rachel just laughed and said that was just the way opera stories were written. Will I die before I get married? No, darling of course not. The stories are silly, just enjoy the music. But you couldn't ignore the story, thought Florrie, because it was part of the music.

When she was 12, her 'Auntie' Leah took her out to a different theatre. This one was in a narrow street in the centre of the city, surrounded by pubs and grown up shops. People were everywhere, some of them a bit drunk and shouting. She had to hang onto Auntie Leah's hand even more tightly. Auntie Leah was not that much older than Florrie (perhaps 19 or 20) and very grown up. To get to the theatre, they turned down a little alley. She could see the entrance with flashing light bulbs and garish posters. It was the notorious City Varieties Music Hall, home of the 'burlesque' show with its saucy singers, raucous comedians and dancing girls with hardly any clothes on. The band was not as impressive as the orchestra at the Grand Theatre but it was bouncy, rhythmic and cheerful. The auditorium was very pretty and Florrie thought it was like being inside her mother's velvet lined jewel box with the precious rings and bracelets glinting and winking at her. The house was full and she was wedged tightly between Auntie Leah and a gentleman with a beard who guffawed loudly at the comedian's jokes and turned with a friendly grin to ask Florrie if she was enjoying herself. Florrie was a little overcome and just nodded shyly, to the gentleman's great delight. The comedians were funny when they did silly dances but they could leer in a frightening way and she couldn't understand all their jokes. There was a man who rode a unicycle and balanced a spinning plate on a pole; and a family of acrobats who were amazing to watch. But she liked the dancing girls best with their silk and satin clothes and their athletic though chubby legs doing such high kicks! And their cheeky smiles. They were so pretty. In the interval they went to the café in the theatre where another gentleman who seemed to be a friend of Auntie's bought her a sherbet drink and biscuits. He had beer in a pint mug and Auntie had a glass of white wine. When the show was over, everyone came up on the stage to bow and say goodbye and they all clapped like mad till Florrie's hands felt sore. On the way home Auntie Leah grew serious and said Florrie, promise me you won't tell your parents where we went. Why not asked innocent Florrie. They may not approve. You know it's a bit racy and some people say not suitable for children. But I'm nearly grown up my Mum protested. I'm twelve. I know, love. I know. But let's not tell them. It'll be our little secret, right?

I must digress briefly about that wonderful little theatre. Florrie didn't know that her parents had been there when they first came to the city. They had seen a similar show that included a clog dancing act by 'The Eight Lancashire Lads', one of whom was the young Charles Chaplin just starting his professional career, and soon to be an emigrant himself. Forty years after Florrie, I would visit the Varieties myself along with my adolescent school friends, all of us eager to see some nearly naked girls. Once a month it would be taken over by the BBC and become respectable, with an evening of old time Music Hall called The Good Old Days, or something like that. I remember that the audience all had to come in Victorian Dress and the show was introduced by a genial and grandiloquent Master of Ceremonies who sat in a stage box with a drink in one hand and a gavel in the other. If you are old enough you may remember those innocent shows which contrasted so memorably with the Varieties' more sleazy weekday performances.

Florrie never told her mother the truth about this episode, but she whispered the story of her adventure to her best friend at school. Her best friend was Ray and the two girls were very close. What did they talk about? Oh, you know the sort of thing: parents, school, other friends, periods, clothes, having to look after younger brothers, boys you liked and boys you didn't like, who might be looking at whom in a special way. This chapter would become a pastiche of the one about Gertie MacDowell and Cissie Caffrey and Edy Boardman in James Joyce's *Ulysses* if I allowed this to go on. But Ray was a very special friend throughout her life. Vigorous and emphatic, enthusiastic about life and books and art; rather plain and destined for a brief marriage ended by her husband's flight from the consequences of white collar crime; but at least he left her a baby who grew up to be a brilliant daughter who got a First in Maths at Oxford and became the first woman leader of Birmingham City Council.

Shortly after the clandestine visit to the Varieties, Florrie had another growing-up experience. The next-door neighbours at 7 Evelyn Street were Mr and Mrs Bergman who were fellow members of the community. Mr Bergman was also Jacob's landlord. When the war broke out more brushes were needed and the bristle business was doing well. The rent was paid punctually and relations between the two families were good. So when the Bergmans asked if their son's fiancée could lodge with Jacob and Rachel for a few months, Florrie's parents readily agreed. Rachel explained to Florrie that the new girl would be sharing her room and her bed and they would become good friends. The new girl was called Irene and she was 16. Irene told her that she was not of our faith but was undergoing conversion so she could marry young Johnny Bergman. Florrie didn't mind sharing her room with Irene and it was fun to have someone to talk to in the same bed. Irene had to get up very early in the morning to go to her tailoring job. Florrie, still in bed and watching her new friend get dressed, would see her squeezing herself into a very tight corset. Soon Irene became very shy about being seen without her clothes on, turning her back on Florrie and slipping quickly into her nightgown. During the night she would have to get up several times to visit the outside toilet in the back yard. Florrie was curious, but Irene was not forthcoming. All the same, she couldn't help noticing that Irene's tummy was getting bigger and that it was quite a struggle for her to do up her buttons.

Eventually Irene became so fat she had difficulty walking about and would have to sit down to get her breath back after climbing the stairs. This was very puzzling and she mentioned it to her mother. Ma, why is Irene so big round the middle? But Rachel just laughed and said perhaps she was eating too much.

Then, one day, when they were sitting doing some sewing in the bedroom, Irene suddenly developed a terrible pain in her tummy and began crying and groaning. After a while Irene calmed down and said the pain had gone. But then it came again, even worse than before and Irene screamed so loudly that Rachel came running up the stairs and threw open the door. She looked at Irene and her face was grim. Grabbing Florrie by the hand she said go into my room at once! Close the door and don't come out till I tell you! Frightened and trembling, Florrie did as she was told. In fact it was a relief to retreat to her parents' room and shut the door on Irene and her pain.

Through the door she could hear the screams continuing with short intervals of quieter sobbing before they started again. She could also hear other voices shouting, doors slamming and people running up and down the stairs. It seemed to go on for ages and she couldn't concentrate on anything to pass the time till she was released. Would Irene be wrapped up and taken to hospital like the boy at her school who had meningitis and was never seen again? Finally the door opened and Rachel came again. Now she was smiling. She took Florrie's hand again and said, now you can go in to Irene and see the baby. The baby was a beautiful little girl with wide eyes and glossy dark hair. Irene held her close and looked at her lovingly. But where had the baby come from? Only grown up women like her mother had babies. Had the pain turned Irene into a grown up? Had the doctor brought the baby so quickly? Would they all live in Florrie's room? Everyone was too excited to tell her, bustling in and out with towels and hot water and cups of tea. But she was allowed to hold the baby and two weeks later, Irene and her fiancé were married in a brief religious ceremony held next door at the Bergmans'. The baby was called Rose. She grew up to be a tall handsome woman with a dignified presence and she married a jovial bookmaker. Shortly after this episode, Jacob and Rachel decided to put some distance between themselves and the Bergmans. They moved to a house in Marlborough Gardens in the even nicer district of Headingley (near the university).

Chapter 5
Matriculation and university life

When Florrie was 16 and-a-half she took her school leaving exams. These were similar to the present GCSE. One difference was that you had to pass in five subjects (including Maths and English) in order to be awarded the Certificate of Matriculation.

This certificate, known as 'Matric', was something really to be proud of as it was the portal to higher education and entitled you to enrol at a university. Florrie was thrilled to get her Matric and pleased that some of her best friends at school had also got through. Jacob and Rachel were intensely proud of their daughter's achievement and were both, for different reasons, happy for her to go on studying. Rachel had more respect for education for its own sake and would have loved to have been a university student herself. Jacob, I am sad to say, thought it would be a waste of time for boys, and he intended his own sons to go straight into the bristle business where their help would be needed if it was to grow. His first idea for Florrie was that she should go to a 'commercial school' to learn shorthand and typing so she could become his secretary. But the places were all reserved for girls who had already left school without qualifications and needed to get jobs. Or so they told Jacob. Still, he thought, the university was fine for a girl. She could study to be a doctor, like Dr Umanski's girl. That was a good idea. At any rate, she could pass the time there until she was old enough to be married, and she would add to her accomplishments. She would meet some of the brightest of the new generation of our people and they might include her future husband. I am afraid that Jacob was no feminist, but in 1918 what could one expect? Women would not get the vote till the war ended and it would still be restricted to those over 30. There were very few women in the professions. Nevertheless, Jacob told Florrie that he thought she should be enrolled at the University of Leeds to study medicine. Still uncertain, she discussed it with her friends.

What sort of friends did the teenage Florrie have? They were the sons and daughters of other immigrant families belonging to our people. Some were a little older and already at the university. Three of them were medics and they seemed to be having a wonderful time. There was Jack Bloom who lived round the corner and was a very good looking, smiling boy. Then there was her cousin Henry. He was the eldest son of Jacob's brother Isaac, now in his fourth year as a medical student. Henry's sweetheart was called Dolly and her father was the greatly admired Dr Umanski, a scholarly man who had been an army doctor in Russia before he arrived in Leeds. Dolly's elder sister, Julia, was also a doctor (as we have heard), having qualified two years earlier. Julia specialised in gynaecology. Florrie was not quite sure what that was but she was full of admiration for Julia who was good looking, confident and knew about all sorts of things.

One evening, Henry, Dolly, Julia and Jack were sitting in Rachel's parlour with Florrie, drinking tea and playing cards.

Suddenly, Julia put down her cards and said, Florrie, have you decided what you are going to study yet? Are you going to do medicine?

The others looked at her expectantly. Julia always came straight out with things like that. She was very direct, for a girl.

It's what Dad thinks I should do, said Florrie. But it must be very hard. And I'm not sure that I could bear to cut up dead bodies.

Ugh, disgusting, said Dolly, pulling a face.

You get used to it, said Henry. But it's not so easy for a girl unless you are tough like Julia.

Julia shook her head. It's not disgusting. It's inspiring and exciting to learn all about the human body, how it's constructed and how it works. There *is* a lot to remember and the Second MB exams are quite tough. But you have a good brain, Florrie.

Florrie blushed with pleasure at the compliment from the wonderful Julia. Listening to them, I have to remind myself that Florrie is still only sixteen; the others are so much more grown up.

Anatomy is only the beginning, said Henry. Wait till you get onto the wards and get a chance to see real live patients! Yesterday Moynihan let me assist him with an appendix. The other fellows were green with envy, I can tell you.

Who is Moynihan? asked Florrie

Berkeley Moynihan. He's our prof of surgery, said Jack who had been waiting for a chance to get Florrie's attention. He's a superb operator and a very good doctor.

A great doctor, said Henry, reverently. It's an honour to be his dresser.

Florrie had a mental picture of Henry helping the great doctor on with his combinations and she smiled to herself. Jack (who was enjoying Florrie's secret smile) explained that students attached to a surgeon were called dressers because traditionally they were supposed to change the patients' dressings, although nowadays the nurses did it.

I'm on a medical firm, Jack went on. We are called 'clerks' because we write down the patient's history. Then we examine them and listen to their hearts and lungs with our stethoscopes. Yesterday I heard a mitral murmur. It's tremendous fun. You must come and join us, Florrie.

Jack was looking forward to the chance of seeing Florrie every day and perhaps becoming her young man.

Are there many lady doctors? Florrie asked Julia.

Not many. But more are coming along. At first the patients couldn't believe I was a doctor. They all thought I was a nurse. But I soon showed them I knew what I was doing. And women really prefer a female doctor, not just to examine them, but to talk to. They prefer a doctor who knows what it is to be a woman.

That night Florrie curled up in her bed and said to herself, I'm going to be a doctor. I'm going to be a lady doctor like Julia. It will be hard work and the bodies will be frightening, but if Henry and Jack can cut them up, I can do it too. And then I shall be a clerk and a dresser and have a stethoscope round my neck. And then I'll visit people in their houses and they'll be glad to see me and I shall make them better.

Tonight she was just a little girl who helped her mother with shopping and cooking and had to put up with cheek from three little brothers. But she had got her Matric! And in a few weeks she would be a grown up student at the university, on her way to becoming a doctor.

❧

The university was a short walk away from Florrie's home in Marlborough Gardens. Today's proud architectural statement, the Parkinson Building, a monument in Portland Stone, was not there in Florrie's day. But there was a redbrick Great Hall, some lecture rooms and a students' union to provide a focus in University Road. Most of the individual departments were housed in adaptations of the surrounding middle class terraced houses. If you were going to study medicine in 1918 you had to start off with a preliminary course called First MB (Bachelor of Medicine). This consisted of physics, chemistry and biology, all of which sciences were a necessary precursor to the study of human anatomy (dissecting bodies) and human physiology (how the living body works in health) which was called Second MB. If you survived the terrible second MB exam and its obsessive demands on the adolescent memory, you were invited into the hospital to meet the patients and the professors of medicine and surgery. You went to lectures on pathology, pharmacology and *materia medica*. You watched doctors at work and you learned to do what they did. After three more years, if you passed Final MB, you were admitted to the degree of MB ChB, which is short, in Latin, for Bachelor of Medicine, Bachelor of Surgery. Nowadays, students stay on at school and do their basic sciences for A level, so First MB has been abolished. Which I think is a pity because it combined studies that were not too taxing with an opportunity to live the life of a student. Perhaps Sixth Form colleges now provide a similar experience.

ço

On a bright, sunny September day Florrie walked eagerly up University Road on her way to register. The Great Hall was crowded with students of both sexes. She was greeted by people she knew and felt she was where she was meant to be. She signed her name half a dozen times; she promised to obey the rules of the University; she enrolled for her courses; she became a paid up member of the Union, and she joined several Societies. She sat with her fellow freshmen and women in a tiered lecture theatre and listened to an address of welcome. She felt proud and exultant to a member of such a company of bright minds. In the cafeteria she was introduced to people, mainly boys but some girls as well. The conversation, she noticed with approval, was completely different from home and school. The students talked about politics; they discussed seriously, and sometimes passionately, the future of England in the post war world. They were concerned about foreign countries too: they believed in a new spirit of international co-operation that would follow the end of the war. Later on, she would remember a day in November when their lecturer was handed a note, and he announced to the class that the Armistice had been signed. The students all shouted with joy, some threw their books in the air and everyone rushed outside to join the celebrations. After that, the former soldiers, those who had survived the trenches, began to appear in the classes and the common rooms also. They were older and had been through experiences they didn't want to talk about. Some declared themselves socialists and looked forward to the day when the workers would govern the country. They talked about the ideas of Freud and Marx and other names that were new to her. She longed to know more and to be able to take part rather than just listening. And as she was an attractive girl there were plenty of young men only too willing to explain things to her. And she did know about some things. She had read the Classic English novels at school and her mother had introduced her to Pushkin and Tolstoy. She was by now a good pianist and she could hold her own in a conversation about music.

Florrie's studies began, not in the medical school which was some distance away, near the Infirmary, but in the science departments in their little houses in University Road. There were lectures, there was laboratory work and there was a lot of reading. She loved the biology which was clearly the first step on the yellow brick road to being a doctor. She loved to learn about the heart and the lungs and the digestive organs. She liked the way the systems of the body cooperated with each other. Even the dissection of the frog and the rabbit ceased to be gruesome once you got involved in finding all their little organs and revealing their functional beauty.

Chemistry was a little more difficult but she could manage it. She liked the variety of the elements and the strange orderliness of the Periodic Table. After some difficulty she mastered the formulae and the equations. Chemistry and biology were fine. But physics was a problem. For a start there was a lot of mathematics which she found very hard, although they kept insisting that it was all common sense. Then there were the experiments which involved strange ungainly pieces of equipment. A wooden contraption with brass screws and coiled up wires, called a Wheatstone Bridge. What was it for? Clocks called galvanometers, with a single hand that jerked in response to electric currents. Long glass tubes attached to each other with dirty orange rubber connections. And always the calculations. What exactly was electricity and why must there be a potential difference? Why were mirrors in the physics lab curved, and why was light represented by spindly lines crossing and recrossing each other? Poor Florrie struggled with physics and felt herself, for the first time in her life, slipping behind the rest of the class.

And so, when the exams came at the end the year, she had a distinction in Biology and a pass in chemistry but she had failed in physics.

She had an interview with the dean who said she could retake it six months later but there would be an extra fee to pay, and she would have to retake the chemistry as well, as they were somehow bound up with each other. This was not explained. Her friends reassured her that she would pass next time; this was merely a little setback. Her parents were clearly disappointed, but her father said she should try again and he was willing to pay the fee. But sadly, something was broken in her by that first academic failure. She felt that she would never pass physics however many times she tried, because it spoke in a language she didn't understand and which it seemed no one could teach her. Thinking about it now, it seems to me to be so sad that nobody was there to encourage her, to say *allez, allez* Florence! You can do it! We will coach you, show you a few tricks for mastering the calculations, get you through to the next stage and get you back on track. I wish I had been there to help. Although I am no great shakes at physics myself, I would have found someone to do the job. But in 1919, there was nobody farsighted enough to help Florrie over the Wheatstone Bridge and back onto the road to a medical career. She just lost heart and lost her academic self-confidence. When she was 95, in the nursing home and with not much of her higher brain still functioning, I sat one day talking to the male nurse who was feeding her. I told him the story. Why did you give up medicine, Florence? he asked her, his spoon poised in the air. Too difficult, was all she could say. It makes me want to weep. My mother could have been a doctor if only I had been there to help her.

Her father sat down with her one evening to talk about it. Jacob is now in his early 40s and rather different from the eager young man we first met in the town of K. He still has the Rostov energy, the bristle merchant briskness, but he has become rather more stern and conservative. He is a successful businessman, a British Citizen since 1909 and the father of four teenagers. He made a big decision to emigrate when he was 21; but can he understand the feelings of his seventeen-year-old daughter?

He starts off grandly.

You can do the exam again. It vill cost tventy pound but I vill pay de money. You vill study hard and you vill pass next time.

Florrie is looking at her feet. Her heart is full of emotion.

Thank you, Dad. But I can't go back.

Vy not?

I just don't think I could do it. However many times I try.

You don't vant any more to be a doctor?

I don't know what I want. I just feel… ashamed of myself. I can't face the lecturers any more. They must think I am such a stupid, stupid girl. And the tears start to well up in her blue eyes.

Jacob sighs deeply. He finds this hard to cope with. He should put his arms round her and give her a hug but somehow he can't do it. He feels an undertow of anger within him. She's let me down, he thinks. Maybe it was all a waste of time and money anyway, trying to make a girl to be a doctor.

If you don't go back, vat vill you do? (Does he mean get married? Her mother thinks she is much too young.)

I don't know. I don't know. I'm no good for anything.

Nonsense! You are upset, that's all. Drink your tea now. Ma and I vill have a talk.

This was a miserable time for Florrie. Perhaps the first of her slides into depression. Her brothers were aware that something had gone wrong. Florrie wasn't going to be a doctor anymore. She wasn't as clever as she was supposed to be. Their initial triumphal feeling was modified by shock at their big sister's diminution and some compassion for her. Harry, only two years younger, wondered how his own chances of going to the university would be affected by this catastrophe. Rachel tried to persuade her to go back and take the exam again but Florrie's face was stony and she refused to discuss it.

Let me try once more to understand what happened. I need to get inside my teenage mother again and experience her feelings. Here we go, through the portal of empathic imagination and back along the umbilical cord. Immediately I can feel the shame and disappointment with herself. She wants to hide herself away. No wonder she doesn't want to listen to all these people giving her advice. What do they know about how she struggled to understand that stuff? Can't go back there, I just can't, she says to me. I don't think I really want to be a doctor, anyway. It's all right for Henry and Julia and the others; but I'm not as clever as them. It was all a mistake. I want them to forget the whole thing; hide myself away and then start again as if it never happened. But, I want to say to her, you like the biology and even the chemistry and the idea of visiting patients in their homes. I know, I know. I would like to have done that. And I feel sad that I never will. Then she smiles at me, her lovely open smile: but you children will do it for me in the end, all of you. Maybe I just had to start you off.

It was painful to face her medical friends. Henry and Julia told her vigorously that she should try again but they soon saw it was useless. Jack Bloom was more sympathetic and said he didn't see why she should have to struggle with physics if she hated it. Maybe she could teach English or music, he suggested. Later on she wistfully wondered why she hadn't changed to biology. But nothing like that ever happened. Student life was over. She continued to have her music lessons and to help her mother at home. After a while, everyone accepted that Florrie wasn't going to be a doctor any more and was just like the other girls they knew. But she continued to be interested in the world around her. She would go round to Jack's house and have supper with him and his parents and his sister. Jack's mother was the secretary of the Women's Homeland Association, dedicated to raising funds for those of our people who wanted to start a new life in the Middle East. One day, said Jack's mother, we shall have our own state, where our ancestors came from. Already we are making the desert bloom. Florrie found the heroic idea of Homeland stirring and she enjoyed the intellectual and political talk in Mrs Bloom's kitchen. She would imagine what it might be like to be a pioneer in the new land, a strong sun-tanned girl working in an orange grove and singing and dancing round a campfire in the evenings. But she never really wanted to go there in person. She wanted to go on being English.

Her best friend, Ray, was also a great help. Like Florrie, she had done well at Matric but her parents were poor and so she had to get a job when she left school. Ray worked in an office at the local branch of the Ministry of Labour, helping other people to find work and assessing their eligibility for the new National Insurance benefit if they were not fit. Florrie and Ray met at each other's houses: they went shopping for clothes together, they went to the pictures. Charlie Chaplin was their favourite, especially when the films got longer and the characters began to tug at your feelings as well as make you laugh. They also liked the romantic films, and they pretended to swoon over Valentino. Of course, the films were not yet talkies, but there was music from a piano or even a little orchestra. In the summer, they would get the tram to the outskirts of the city and go for long country walks. In cinematic terms this would be a montage of their activities as the years slowly passed. Florrie is seventeen and then eighteen. She and her girl friends are talking more about boys and marriage. Ray has an understanding with a rather brilliant young solicitor. Unhappily, it will all go wrong, as I mentioned earlier. Florrie had some admirers, such as Jack, but had so far given no one any encouragement to take the next step. This was shortly to change, partly because of her parents' new attitude.

By the end of 1921, Rachel and Jacob had come round to thinking that it was time for Florrie to get married. She was well aware that there were more visitors to the house in Marlborough Gardens and some of them were quite reasonable looking young men. One day, she overheard her father saying to a visiting cousin from the old country: *my daughter is my problem now.* She felt hurt and angry with him for calling her a problem and she knew he was talking about 'getting her off'. What business had they to try and get her off with some man? On the other hand, some of the young men were quite attractive and she could imagine being kissed by one of them and then having a wonderful wedding and a house of her own with her new husband. Among the visitors were the Levinskys, young Bertie and his pretty sister Laura, who used to come over from Dewsbury, about 10 miles away. The Levinskys were a wealthy family (or so her parents told each other). They were in the clothing trade, like most of our people, but they were smarter than most and had made a lot of money through government contracts for soldiers' uniforms during the war. They had two shops in Dewsbury, run by the father and three sons and were reported to be doing very well.

One afternoon, soon after her 20th birthday, Florrie was planning to go out to a Homeland meeting when her father beckoned her aside and told her she must stay in because there was a visitor coming who he wanted her to meet. Jacob was quite an authoritarian father now, as I have indicated, and Florrie felt she had to obey him. Besides, she was curious to see what sort of boy he had lined up for her.

Chapter 6
Courtship – marriage – conflict – insecurity

And so my father walks into the story. His name is Emanuel Levinsky but he is always called Manny. He is about 5 foot 8 inches tall, with dark, straight, brylcream-smooth hair and he is good looking. Florrie likes him from the start. She offers him tea and a cake, and they chat on the settee in the parlour. Manny is a good listener. She finds herself telling him about having to give up the university. He is sympathetic. He would like to have gone there himself, only there was not enough money and then the war came. He has three brothers and three sisters. Florrie already knows his younger sister Laura who has a good singing voice. Manny is the third oldest. He tells her he is 26, nearly 7 years older than Florrie. They talk about the films they have seen and the new dance hall that has just opened. He is a keen footballer and is the secretary of his local club. He jokingly invites Florrie to come and watch a match and she jokingly agrees, although she would rather go to the pictures. She asks if he likes music and he says he plays the violin a little, but prefers to listen. They are getting on very well. When they have a little laugh together his arm slips briefly round her waist and she likes that, because her parents are not very good at showing affection physically.

Meanwhile, Rachel and Jacob are talking to Manny's sister and brother and a friend of Rachel's. Every so often, they take a quick glance at Florrie and Manny and they are pleased with what they see. It's going well. She likes him. This will lead to a marriage.

At about 9.30 p.m. the Levinskys excuse themselves. They have to catch the bus back to Dewsbury. But they will come again. Florrie and Manny exchange smiles as they part and think about how to arrange their next meeting. They have each other's telephone numbers. (Leeds was an early beneficiary of automatic dialling.) When her parents ask her if she enjoyed the evening, Florrie says yes. And what did she think of Manny? asks her mother. He seems very nice, she says, trying to give nothing away, and her parents beam.

In bed, that night, Jacob and Rachel discuss their prospective son-in-law. Can he provide for their daughter? That's an important question for these parents who have struggled up from poverty and insecurity only recently. It's a good business, says Jacob. They did very well in the war, making uniforms for the soldiers. Now they have two shops, both doing nicely. Suits and ladies' costumes made to measure, very good quality. Even fur coats they will make for you. They supply the cloth and they take the measurements but they are not cutters and pressers themselves. It's all contracted out, the work. It's much better than slaving away in the shop yourself.

He's a nice kind boy as well, says Rachel. Everyone says so. He will look after her.

What is Florrie thinking now? We know that she was resentful of the plans to get her off. But having met and talked to the chosen fiancé, her anger softened and was replaced by an eager feeling that life was about to get better. Something good was within her reach. Her female physiology (which she had only briefly learned about at the University) was functioning normally. She was attracted to good-looking, personable young men. She liked the way they looked at her with admiration and desire. She knew what it meant and in some cases she responded. With Manny she responded. She liked his thick black hair and his warm smile. She looked forward to their first kiss which would come soon, she felt sure.

Now, you will appreciate that this part is becoming difficult for your narrator. I like to get (back) inside my heroine and feel her hormones washing over me, letting me in on her girly emotions. But at the same time a voice within me protests that this is too close. Soon my parents are going to start having sex. I shouldn't really be here; I should be asleep in my own bedroom. It's none of my business.

It is the following evening. The telephone rings in 7, Marlborough Gardens. I'll get it, cries alert Florrie, her heart thumping in her breast. She dashes into the hall and picks up the receiver. It is Manny! Would she like to come to the theatre to see a Gilbert and Sullivan opera: HMS Pinafore? He has tickets for Thursday (today is Monday). Of course she would. She reins in the eagerness in her voice, just a little. That would be lovely. Thank you so much. He will pick her up at 7 o'clock if that is all right. I'll say it's all right.

Now I remember the four blue hard-backed volumes of Gilbert and Sullivan songs with words and piano score which sat on the top shelf of the cloakroom in the house where I was born 19 years later. I remember Florrie in her forties, sitting at the piano in our tasteful but chilly 'lounge'. She is playing and singing 'Little Buttercup' from *HMS Pinafore*:

'For I'm called Little Buttercup – Dear Little Buttercup,
Though I could never tell why,
But still I'm called Buttercup, poor Little Buttercup,
Sweet Little Buttercup I!'

I am about six. I am aware that it is a nice tune and that she sings well. I have no idea who Buttercup is, unless it is a name she has for herself. It's one of my really nice memories of my Mum. I may tell you later about other songs she sang. But what did it mean to her?

Serious musicians often have a low opinion of Gilbert and Sullivan, and it doesn't count as proper opera. But Florrie used to sing and play 'Buttercup', and other Savoy opera songs, and when I hear them performed in the theatre, my eyes unaccountably start watering. It can be quite uncomfortable. This cheap music seems to mean a lot to me, so I guess that it meant a lot to her too, and that it started with that first hot date with Manny in 1922 at the Leeds Grand Theatre and Opera House. A touring production with probably a small orchestra. Maybe the London principals didn't come. No matter. They sat in the front row of the upper circle. His arm went round her, making her shiver with pleasure and this time it stayed round. In the second half they held hands. When the curtain came down at the end, she turned her face towards him to thank him, and they kissed... (There, I've done it. They are kissing and they are both feeling full of love and desire and I'm still there.)

I am reminded, not for the first time, of a short story by the American writer Delmore Schwartz, first published in 1937. It is called 'In Dreams Begin Responsibilities'. When the story begins, the narrator is watching a silent, rather scratchy black and white film set in 1909 and showing images of his parents before their marriage. I think you can see why this story appeals to me. The narrator (who is on the eve of his 21st birthday) can also hear his young father's thoughts and feelings. As he watches the film, he becomes increasingly disturbed. He sees his mother and father meeting, talking and walking arm and arm on the seaside board walk at Coney Island. They go in to a restaurant and, to the strains of an intoxicating waltz, he asks her to marry him. At this point the young man stands up in the cinema and shouts out, 'Don't do it. It's not too late to change your minds, both of you. Nothing good will come of it, only remorse, hatred, scandal and two children whose characters are monstrous.' Now I have no wish to intervene retroactively in the course of history. My parents' marriage was by no means a disaster and good things did come out of it. There were three children, not two, and none of us was monstrous. So when I see them about to take the big step I am all for it, urging them on if anything. And even the character in the story becomes anxious, later on in the film, that his parents will lose each other and not get married after all. This is even more terrifying. No, it's not that I want to stop them, but I see them on the brink of a life together that will have more anxiety and yes, heartbreak is not too strong a word, than the poor young things can possibly imagine. The other matter, the embarrassing fact that they are going to have sex, I think I can handle. I rather enjoy their kissing and putting their arms round one another affectionately. It makes me feel secure. I wish I had seen more of it when the three of us were together.

As for the sex, the more intimate mingling of their bodies, as for that, I am pretty sure they did not get that far until they were married. I think I prefer it that way. When I first began to learn the details of human sexual intercourse I worked out that, as we were three children, they probably just did it three times. I allowed them a few more goes because not every act of love would result in a child and there was no reason they should not get some pleasure out of their failed attempts to produce us children. It was only later that I had to concede that they probably did it quite a lot, just for pleasure and because they desired each other and even used whatever was available at the time to prevent

46

their pleasure resulting in more children. These pre-adolescent ideas are amusing now; but there is still something a little awesome about being present, even in my imagination, when my parents are behaving like everybody else and having sex.

Further dates followed quickly. They went dancing at the Mecca Dance Hall in the elaborately decorated County Arcade. They went to the cinema, where they could hold hands in the dark and feel the warm weight of each other's bodies. Manny became a regular visitor in Marlborough Gardens where he was now accepted as Florrie's intended. She went to Dewsbury to meet his family. His brother Eli was the only one to serve in the war. He had gone down with malaria and still suffered outbreaks of fever; Manny told her that had to be treated with quinine. The others had not been to the war and she wondered why not, but didn't like to ask. There was a younger brother (Bertie) who was lively and friendly. Manny and Bertie worked together at one of the family's two tailoring shops. The sisters were Amelia (tall and stately) Rose (a schoolteacher, easy to get on with) and the youngest, the quiet Laura, whom Florrie liked best. She noticed that they were all quite different from the Rostovs. Her father was vigorous, forthright in his opinions and impatient of any alternative viewpoints. He made decisions quickly and tended to support the Conservative party who supported Business. Her eldest brother, Harry, now 18, was a younger model of their father. Abe, with his bad leg, was gentler and more reflective but could still come out with very definite opinions. And Benny tried his best to keep up with Harry.

The Levinskys, in contrast, seemed to float through life in a whimsical sort of way. They had gentle smiles and were never in a hurry, always willing to sit and chat. Their house, though large, was not as well furnished as her own.

And so, on October 31st, they were married. The service was in the Great Synagogue in Belgrave Street off Chapeltown Road and the reception at the Lyons' Arcadia Rooms in the Victorian County Arcade. All their friends and their relatives from both families came to the reception. They were given many presents which would last them for the greater part of their married life. There were dinner services, canteens of posh cutlery, lace tablecloths, linen for a double bed, all the things that a young couple setting up house would need. Harry, Abe and Benny clubbed together and bought their sister a large wooden 'mangle' that looked like a piece of machinery from the industrial revolution. It had two large wooden rollers, turned by an iron handle by way of a system of giant oily cogwheels. Florrie regarded it with mixed feelings; she appreciated that they had spent their money on her, but their choice seemed to be a symbol of domestic servitude.

The young couple moved into a terrace house with indoor plumbing at no. 6 Grange Crescent in Chapeltown. Jacob paid the deposit and the monthly payments came out of Manny's wages. The business remained in Dewsbury, and every day Manny would get a bus into the City centre and then stand under a gloomy railway arch with trains thundering overhead to catch another bus for the ten-mile trip to work. In the shop, he and Bertie would wait for customers to come through the door in search of a new suit or a costume for the wife. Maybe a fur coat for the more prosperous wives. When a customer came in, Manny would listen to his requirements and then show him some 'books' of cloth samples. When he had made his choice, which could take a long time, his measurements were taken: chest, waist, hips arm length, inside leg length and so on, everything carefully noted down. The cloth was then ordered from the wholesalers in Leeds and brought home in a carefully wrapped brown paper parcel tied up with thick, hairy string. The next day he would take the parcel of cloth back to Dewsbury, and deliver it to a tailoring workshop along with the measurements. Manny was on good terms with the master tailors who ran these establishments. They were rather better than the sweatshops of the beginning of the century, but it was still hard work with long hours for the army of cutters, machinists, buttonholers, padders and pressers who could be heard in the back of the shop. When the suit or the coat was ready Manny would be round again to collect it. Back in his own shop he would unwrap the clothes and make sure they looked neat and well pressed for the customer when he came for a fitting. Usually there was a halfway stage at which the components of a suit were only loosely assembled for the preliminary fitting. Alterations were easy to make at this stage and Manny and Bertie would redraw the lines where the stitching would be with large triangular pieces of chalk. Finally the suit would be ready and, if all had gone well, the customer would be delighted. If you are interested in seeing the bespoke tailor in action I can recommend, perhaps surprisingly, the 1932 musical film *Love Me Tonight*, starring Maurice Chevalier and Jeanette MacDonald and directed by the legendary genius of mobile camerawork, Rouben Mamoulian. I shall return to this film a little later on because it has for me a powerful resonance with the life of my parents and their relationship with the Rostovs.

Into Manny's shop in 1922 came a trickle of customers, but not a flood. Just enough to make a living for the young couple and pay the mortgage. For the wartime boom in clothing was over. Uniforms were no longer required. The economy was sagging quite badly and jobs were being lost. Unemployed people couldn't afford new clothes. Many of the middle class men, who were the majority of their customers, were now getting their clothes 'off the peg': ready-made by the multiple tailors like Montague Burton, whose shops were appearing in both Leeds and Dewsbury. If the new suit was not an exact fit, the big store's tailors would do alterations. The clothes were much cheaper, and who could tell the difference? Only a professional.

In the new year (1923) the Levinsky tailoring business faced a new crisis. The council wanted to widen the road where Manny and Bertie's shop was situated and this meant demolishing the building. They were offered a new site but they would have to buy the land and pay for the new building. There wasn't enough money. Manny's father had an emergency conference with his three sons. The majority view was that they would have to abandon Manny and Bertie's shop and all work from the other one. But Manny wanted to hang on to his own shop in the hope that business would pick up. Where could he get the money? Florrie said she would ask her parents if they could help.

We can now eavesdrop on a scene in Jacob and Rachel's new home in Chapeltown (they had moved again after Florrie's marriage). Money was of course a matter to be discussed between men in those days. Jacob was a little surprised to find that the wealthy Levinskys were not in a position to take advantage of the opportunity to have a brand new shop; but he could see that putting up the money himself would be a good investment.

Now, Manny, says Jacob, I understand dey are videning the road and your shop vill come down. You can build a new one, but you don't have the gelt. So you vant a little help. Now, is it in a good part of town?

Oh yes, says Manny eagerly. It's on the corner of a new shopping arcade leading from the High Street down to the market. And we will be on the High Street corner where everyone can see us.

His heart is pounding a little but he tries not to show his anxiety. Old Rostov is a tough customer, and he isn't going to part with money easily. Manny can sense his disappointment that his son-in-law should have to come to him for money and not to his own family. On the other hand, he will want to do the best for his daughter.

He shows Jacob the architect's pictures of the new development.

Verra nice, says Jacob. Now show me de figures. How much vill you need?

It's £1000 for the site and another £1000 for Manny's contribution to the building, plus the cost of fitting and furnishing the new shop, which will have storerooms and offices on the floor above. £2500 in all. It doesn't sound much, I know, but in 1922 it must have been huge...

Jacob makes his decision quickly. I'll pay for your new shop. But I do it because you are my daughter's husband. I vant to look after her and her children. (Manny winces at this harsh exclusion of himself but says nothing.) The property vill be in my daughter's name. You can have it for your business. But only you and Florrie. The rest of your family vill not have an interest. You understand?

Manny understands. His family are being admonished for their lack of ability to weather the depression. Only because he is married to Florrie is he alone of the Levinskys to be allowed to shelter under the Rostov umbrella. But he is also very relieved. Back in Grange Crescent, Florrie is waiting to hear the result of the meeting. She doesn't like this new coolness between the two important men in her life. It is unsettling. Her father is always right and has vast business experience. But she is also fiercely loyal to her man, her Manny. It hurts her to see the look of contempt in her father's eyes when he heard that Manny would need help to buy the new premises.

But when Manny gets back he is looking pleased with himself.

It's going to be all right, he says. We can have the money. Your father will pay for it all. And the property will be in your name. To give you security.

Can't you give me security? asks Florrie. If my dad and my brothers can make enough money, why can't you?

And she starts to cry. My poor father tries to comfort her, but she shakes him off. He hasn't seen her like this before. He tries to explain. There is a slump. Business is bad everywhere. People are unemployed and can no longer afford to spend money on new clothes. When they have to buy a new suit they go to the multiple tailors who can do off-the-peg suits in cheap materials at knockdown prices. Very few people want proper made-to-measure suits any more, and so the bespoke tailor finds it hard to make a living. Florrie dries her eyes and allows his arm to go round her shoulders.

Even with the new shop, how will we manage? She looks tearfully up at him.

We can rent part of it out. And we have some new ideas. We can sell cheap Telemark raincoats. And better off people are still buying fur coats for their wives... We can advertise in the paper that we make fur coats. I'm going to talk to the furriers tomorrow. We'll be all right.

But in his heart, he's not so sure. Because the other brothers are worried. They and his father are talking about closing the other shop and going to work as tailors for Burton or Hepworth who are taking on more cutters and machinists.

On Sunday they go round to the Rostovs. Florrie goes straight to the kitchen to help Rachel with the dinner. Manny goes into the parlour with Jacob and finds Florrie's brothers there. All three of them are now working for the family business, J. Rostov and sons, Bristle Merchants. Harry is now a man of 20 and looks like a young edition of his father but without the moustache. He greets Manny rather coldly. Abe, who is 18, is more friendly and relaxed. Benny the youngest brother takes his cue from Harry.

So your business is not doing so well? says Harry.

Nobody is doing well at present, says Manny. It's the slump.

Well, the bristle business is all right, says Harry.

I suppose there is still a demand for brushes. But not for well-made clothes.

You did all right in the war, says Benny.

I know. That was because of the uniforms. Now that's all finished.

Well, that was obviously going to happen, says Harry. But if you know about business, you can adapt to the market conditions.

That's why we are successful, says Benny. And you are not.

Be quiet, Benny, says his father.

He has a point, says Harry. We were hoping for a better future for our sister. Look, Manny, we were told that your business was sound and that Florrie would be well provided for. Now we are not so sure. Manny is a mild, easy-going sort of chap but he has difficulty keeping cool in the face of this attitude from his brothers in law. Jacob sees that the tension is rising and moves in to call off his sons.

That's enough, he says. Dey vill have de shop, now. It's a good investment and it's in Florrie's name so she vill be secure. Soon, ven conditions improve, der vill be more money in der pockets and your trade vill pick up.

Benny now tries to ease the atmosphere by asking about how Manny's football team have been doing this season. Rachel comes in and tells them dinner is ready.

Dinner is uncomfortable. Florrie can hardly bear it. She has heard raised voices from the parlour and she can tell from the frigid atmosphere in the dining room, and the way her brothers look at her husband, that they have only contempt for him. A psychoanalyst might say that they were also jealous that he had taken their lovely sister away from them. They could be right. But psychoanalysts will have their turn a little later in this story.

1923 moved in to 1924. Have the young couple got past this episode of conflict and unpleasantness? Yes and no. I am certainly feeling uneasy myself for several reasons.

They had their own house with plenty of space. They even had a living-in maid, which even people of their relatively low income did in those days. In Dewsbury, a smart new arcade is being built with Manny's shop (or perhaps we should say Florrie's shop) occupying a prominent place on the corner with the High Street. Manny was getting a few orders for suits and also selling some raincoats. They were getting by without having to ask for any more help from Jacob Rostov. They could still enjoy their outings on the town to cinemas, theatres and dance halls. They had Florrie's friends. She is a sociable girl. Manny doesn't have many friends of his own apart from a couple of fellows he has lunch with, once a week in Dewsbury. He is no longer involved with the football club. But he likes her friends, well-educated, lively, mainly single women, and they like him. And they have each other. At weekends they continued to go to her parents and there things are not so good for Manny. There are no recriminations any more; although at some point, Jacob will always enquire how business is going, as if further collapse was bound to happen sooner or later (in which he was correct). Florrie's brothers maintain a lofty rather satirical attitude to the man who had taken away their sister. Manny hates this, but he keeps quiet, for Florrie's sake.

What is making me uneasy? I don't like having to paint such an unkind picture of my Rostov uncles. Am I being unfair to them? I was always very fond of them, and they were good to me. But, even I could pick up the condescension in their attitude to my dad when they came to call. I tended to agree with the version that my gentle, good-natured father was not in the same class as the powerful charismatic Rostov brothers.

I feel a ridiculous sense of shame that Manny didn't become a soldier in the War. His brother Eli joined up (probably conscripted) but the other three boys didn't. Were they excused on health grounds? Or because the government didn't want to risk the lives of every member of a family? Or because they were needed to go on producing those uniforms that my father helped to make, but never wore. In fact, he told me that they paid some money secretly to someone, and their conscription papers never came. I tell myself that this was a sensible thing to do. The war was monstrous and pointless. If Manny had joined up there is a high probability that he would have been killed, never have married Florrie, and I wouldn't be writing this now because I would never have existed. And yet, I feel deeply ashamed that my Dad didn't do his bit. I can feel the Rostov contempt in my own heart. At the same time, I want to defend and protect him.

Chapter 7
Financial crisis

Now we are well into 1924. The Labour Party have formed a government. They don't have a parliamentary majority and they will last only a few months before the other parties gang up on them; but it's a start. Manny, who has voted for them, is thrilled that the working man's party is at last in charge and able, perhaps, to make some changes. The Rostovs, staunch Conservatives, are dismayed. Florrie can't vote yet because she is under 30. She is privately pleased that Labour are in power but doesn't attempt to debate politics with her father and brothers. She leaves that to Manny who tells them he is a Communist. They laugh and tell him he is naïve and knows nothing about business but privately they are rather shocked.

As Ramsay MacDonald and his colleagues grapple with the teetering economy, Florrie has some exciting news. She has missed two periods and started to feel different. She has been to the doctor who confirmed that she is pregnant. She is filled with pride, excitement and a new sense of purpose. If she can't be a doctor, she will be a biologist, bringing new life into the world. She will have a career as a mother. When she tells Manny, he is delighted and gives her a big hug. He likes the idea of being a father. Fatherhood will also distance him from the young Rostovs who are still only boys despite their confidence and swagger. But before his first baby is born, life has further anxieties in store for my father. Orders for suits and coats are dwindling away to nothing. What can he do? He doesn't want to give up and go back to being an employee. Or try selling things pathetically from door to door as some of the former war heroes are doing. He sits in the front room pondering the fate of his little family. All that money the Rostovs have spent on his new shop and yet he can't attract any customers. They will despise him even more. Nowadays they would say he was a loser. There are equally crushing words to expressing their contempt in the language of the old country and he can hear them in his head. Then he has a bright idea. He owns the shop but he doesn't really need all that space. He can retreat to the office upstairs (just until the slump is over) and rent out the ground floor with its generous curved window commanding the corner of high street and arcade. He begins to compose the advertisement in his head.

It was a good idea in principle but there were problems. Potential tenants responded to his advertisement in the *Dewsbury Chronicle* and in the shop window. A succession of hopeful traders tried to sell ready-made clothes, shoes, household goods and stationery. None of them could make it pay. The slump obstinately remained. Unemployment was high, few people had money to buy anything new, and after a few months, the tenants moved. The last one stayed but didn't pay any rent for three months despite Manny's attempts to persuade him. He was a friend of the Rostovs, which made things more difficult. In the end, the tenant's solicitor telephoned Manny and advised him to give up. He's got no money, chuckled the solicitor, stating the obvious. Black clouds began to gather. Manny had less to give Florrie for her housekeeping. Their outings were strictly limited. Then he came home one day and told her that he thought he might be going bankrupt. There would be a meeting of his creditors to decide whether they would force this to happen. It sounded terrible and Florrie was badly frightened. Who were these creditors, solemnly putting her husband on trial? Her Dad would never allow this to happen to his business. She shouldn't have said that, but I'm afraid she did. The threat of poverty scared her and affected her loyalty.

As they lay in bed at night she would go over and over their predicament, picturing the worst that could happen, convinced that it would.

We will have no money to pay the mortgage. The bailiffs will come banging on the door. I've seen it happen, Manny, in the Leylands. We'll be out on the street with all our furniture and our clothes. And me with the baby coming. Suppose I lose the baby?

And the disgrace. How can I face my brothers? What will my father say? He and Ma will have to take us in. They will say I never should have married you.

Manny, who has been trying to sleep, turns over to her and says, your father has plenty of money. He could help us out with the payments until business gets better.

Oh, you would think of that! Just go to my father again, cap in hand like a *shnorrer* (beggar). Already they have bought the shop for me. At least I have some security there. And as soon as things go wrong, you want to go back for more money. I am so ashamed.

And she begins to sob. Manny's heart is gripped by icy fingers. He tries to keep control of his own emotions. He loves Florrie but he doesn't like this side of her, the way she turns away from him when life gets difficult. Perhaps it's the baby coming that makes her so frightened; but why does she have to blame him? Why can't they be like partners and friends, fighting life's battles together?

I would like to see Florrie reacting in a different, more positive way. Like this for example:

Who were these creditors, solemnly putting her husband on trial?

There must be some way we can find the money, she says. Perhaps we could go to Uncle Isaac for a loan, until times get better. I don't want to go to my father, after the way he spoke to us last time. He'll say he bought us the shop and now we haven't been able to get a tenant for it, we want more money.

I'm sorry this has happened, love, says Manny. I never expected things to get so bad. Sometimes I sit in the office all day and nobody comes. I feel I've let you down.

Listen, it's not your fault. You're a good, hard-working man and you've done your best. Times are bad for everyone. I wish I could help earn some money. Ray goes out to work in the pensions office every day. I should have done that too. I can still learn to type.

But the baby, the baby is coming. You wouldn't be able to work. Of course I could, for a few months. And after that maybe I could do something at home. Some sort of secretarial work. Or anything. We could sell some of our wedding presents. We don't need all this furniture. (But she feels a sharp pang at the thought of her dining room table and chairs being removed. I think of Dr Lydgate's Rosamond in *Middlemarch*.)

You're a good wife, Florrie to want to help. You're a real pal. But I don't want you to have to work. I'll see if I can get a loan from the bank. Or when we have the creditors' meeting I might be able to persuade them to let us pay them off just a little at a time.

We'll both think of things we can do to get us through. I'm so glad I married you. So long as we're together we'll find a way. Now give me a hug and let's get some sleep. We can think about what we are going to do in the morning. Mmmh, that's nice. My big strong husband. Goodnight darling.

Goodnight, sweetheart.

My brother Kenneth prefers that version and I have to say I find it very appealing too. Maybe there were some days when her more generous feelings prevailed over anxiety and anger. So that scene can stay in the director's cut along with original version. But my impression is that the bitterness and anxiety were always waiting to return as soon as there was another setback.

Happily, a few days later, Manny has a stroke of luck. The downstairs shop has been empty for two weeks but suddenly someone wants to rent it, someone whose business is flourishing. A Mr Weston calls at Manny's office. He is a manager for the firm of Wigfall and Sons who have a number of shops in Sheffield and are looking to expand into nearby Yorkshire towns. Wigfall and Sons started off selling bicycles, but now they have diversified into the new Wireless sets, which are getting very popular indeed. The British Broadcasting Company, headed by John Reith, started regular broadcasting a year ago and 'listening-in' is becoming the latest craze. Only a few months earlier, half a million people had heard the voice of King George the Fifth, opening the British Empire Exhibition at Wembley. The royal voice had hitherto been known only within Buckingham Palace. The wireless gave people entertainment in their homes. As well as news and serious talks, they could hear dance music, comedy and sports commentaries. A journalist predicted that soon people would be walking around listening-in with their earphones! They weren't buying new clothes but they weren't to be deprived of the wireless. Mr Weston likes Manny's shop because of its ample space and its commanding position. He is sure they will attract lots of customers, and sell plenty of wireless sets as well as bicycles. He and Manny agreed a rental, which was confirmed in writing from Wigfalls' head office. Soon the downstairs shop would have bright new placard proclaiming the joys of radio. The shelves would be full crystal sets, two valve sets and state-of-the art six valve sets. Wigfalls' became a Dewsbury institution and the rent was always paid on time. As he walked to the nearby bus station, Manny felt joy and triumph for the first time since Florrie had agreed to marry him. That must have been such a good day for him. I wish I had been there when he put his key in the door and said I'm home, Florrie! Guess what's happened! She was pleased, of course. She softened and relaxed and the nicer warm side of her was allowed to come out again, banishing for the time being, the obsessive worrier and faultfinder. They did a little dance around the kitchen together. Thanks to Wigfalls, security had returned. The creditors could be paid and there would be no need for a Meeting. They would keep the house; they would not be put out on the street. They would not have to go to her father like shnorrers. She even felt proud of Manny. He was a businessman after all. He had done a good deal with Wigfalls and was going to take care of her and baby.

Now that the financial crisis has been averted, we can have a pause for reflection. Florrie, what is going in on that little heart of yours? Why don't you have more strength of character? Why don't you stand by your man? Well, you did stand by him, I will concede, for 52 years of marriage, ending only in his death, and I don't think you were ever unfaithful in the technical sense. But you certainly had little faith in your abilities as a couple to work through your problems together. What happened to your strength of character? Where is the brave girl who was a happy student, chatting to all the boys and studying to be a doctor? Talking about politics and books. Playing the piano for them. A girl pretty enough to turn all the men's heads and with the world at her feet. Did that exam failure knock the stuffing out of you? How did you get to be so afraid of insecurity and lack of money? Someone has to look after you. Is that what your Dad told you? He is the powerful influence, your Svengali. You will never be safe without me or someone just as strong and protective as me. You love Dad very much, but you love Manny too, though perhaps less than he loves you. If there is any sign of conflict between Dad and Manny, you run back to Daddy for safety and join in the contemptuous chorus of the Rostovs. He can't give her security. He's not a businessman. He's nothing but a tailor!

The phrase reminds of that film *Love Me Tonight* that I mentioned earlier. When I first saw it I realised with astonishment and delight that it was a romanticised version of *my parents' story*. Delmore Schwartz would have understood perfectly. The film is a musical starring Maurice Chevalier, the French-accented, jaunty young man about Paris with his straw hat and his naughty, suggestive way with a song. In *Love Me Tonight*, Maurice is playing a tailor (called 'Maurice'). His Paris shop is not very different from my father's place in Dewsbury. (Those Hollywood producers, many of whom had emigrated from Russia themselves, would have known all about tailoring.) We see Maurice trying on suits for his customers. He seems very happy with his life. Then, an aristocratic client turns out to be broke and can't pay for the large number of clothes he has ordered. Maurice sets out to track him down in his country chateau and present his bill. On the way, he meets a beautiful and haughty princess played by his regular Hollywood co-star, Jeanette MacDonald who had a perfectly tuned light soprano voice, even if her vocal style now seems dated. No matter. When I see her driving her pony and gig through the woods singing 'Lover when you're near me' I am entranced.

Maurice is smitten too, and tries to charm her with a cheeky song ('Mimi') which she is unable to resist entirely, though she tries hard. When he arrives at the Chateau, Maurice's unreliable customer persuades him to pass himself off as his friend, 'the Baron'. To his surprise the Princess is there too, part of the family ruled over by her uncle, the formidably crusty old Duke. They are all intimidatingly snobbish and class-obsessed. And if you think the French got over all that with their revolution, remember Marcel Proust and his friends. As 'the Baron', Maurice proceeds to charm the whole household and becomes everybody's friend. The Princess, at first aloof, eventually falls in love with him. I think you will understand where I am going with this once you see Florrie as a sort of Rostov Princess. And I guess that's what she was, because to the end of her life people thought there was something aristocratic about her. In the last act of the movie, Maurice offers to remodel the Princess's unflattering riding habit into something more stylish and attractive. He takes her measurements and notes them down just as I remember Manny used to do. He does the job all too well and has to confess that he is not a Baron but a tailor. The Duke and his entire household are furious at the way they have been deceived by the interloper. The portrait of an ancestor falls from the wall in its outrage, intoning in a sepulchral bass: 'the son-of-a-gun is nothing but a tailor!' This phrase is taken up and becomes the refrain of a song that is started by the Duke and passed round the whole supporting cast of relatives and servants.

The film is of course a comedy. It is a comic treatment of the story of how Jacob Rostov, the Duke of Marlborough Gardens, and his family, felt themselves tricked and deceived by that Son-of-a-Gun, my father. And what about the princess? She too gives way to expressions of loathing and disgust at having been tricked by a commoner, a mere tailor. And only a few minutes earlier she was singing like a nightingale of her undying love for him. This is a low point. But a comedy must have a happy ending. She has a miraculous change of heart! She runs out to the stables, flings herself on her horse and gallops off in pursuit of the train that is taking the dejected Maurice back to Paris. When the driver won't stop, she jumps off her horse and stands defiantly on the track facing the engine, which stops just in time. She is brave, she is fearless! She knows what she wants and whom she wants! The lovers are re-united, snobbery is forgotten, she will be a tailor's wife. I wonder if Florrie and Manny saw that picture when it came out in 1932. I know they both liked Maurice Chevalier. Did they see it as their own story, with a moral lesson for princess Florrie?

Chapter 8
First baby; an ill child; nervous breakdown

Financial security has been restored to the Levinsky household although the trauma has left a few scars. Florrie's pregnancy proceeds uneventfully through the rest of 1924 and, in the New Year, on the 20th of January, the day before her own birthday, she gives birth, at home, to their first child, a boy. They call him Michael Samuel and they dote on him. He has fair hair and blue eyes like his mother. Jacob and Rachel are also very pleased with their first grandchild. Florrie's brothers come to visit and crowd round the baby's cot. They are young men now aged 20, 18 and 16. Harry has had a number of girl friends. Benny is taking an interest too. But Abe has held back, self-conscious and ashamed of his awkward gait and his lack of masculine bravado. They are all grudgingly impressed with Manny's achievement in fertilising their sister and making her bring forth this baby. They like the idea of being Uncles.

Michael sucks milk from Florrie's breasts and she loves that. She fondly watches him grow and develop. He smiles, he sits, he crawls. Soon he is taking a few staggering steps. But then he begins to disclose some worrying health problems. His fair skin becomes covered with red papules and rough scaly patches. He itches and rubs his poor little uncomfortable self and cries piteously. Florrie wants to cry too. She tries to comfort her little son but feels powerless to help him. His raw red skin seems to reproach her. If only she had become a doctor! Manny decides to send for Dr Samuel. He too is from the old country and is respected by everyone including the Rostovs. He examines the naked baby and seems neither surprised nor dismayed. Eczema, he calls it, an allergic sensitivity of the skin. He prescribes ointments and advises Florrie about which foods to avoid and how to dress him. The worst areas, his elbows and the backs of his knees will be bandaged by the nurse whom he will send in after him. It will all go away in time, he promises, reassuring the anxious parents with a professional smile.

Little Michael is anointed with thick white zinc oxide paste and castor oil cream.

When this is ineffective a strong smelling coal tar preparation is added which stains everything brown. He is grotesquely bandaged like a half-wrapped mummy and does his best to continue normal infant activities. He is given a sedative medicine to cool his burning skin and stop him scratching. Gradually the flames die down; his skin reverts to something like normal though still very dry. Florrie mourns the lost innocence of his soft white baby skin before the eczema. We know now that eczema is one of the consequences of what immunologists call an atopic tendency. It's the result of an excess of certain antibodies which become paranoid and attack the body's own skin cells. We pour emollients over eczema babies' skins to keep them from drying and apply powerful steroids to quell the inflammatory reaction. Even so there are still some infants who have had it badly like my brother did. Their skin boils and bubbles and is riven with fissures which they try to scratch even deeper. They have to be sedated and bandaged. Their parents are devastated. But they grow out of it, just as the doctors promise. I even had it myself to a milder extent (Yes, it runs in families, there is a gene or two for it). But there is an associated immunological disorder, which follows on its heels and can be life threatening, as it closes down the airways and may cause death.

Now Michael is half-way through his second year. He walks. He laughs, he claps his hands, he babbles and chatters, imitating the grownups' speech. His eczema has subsided but he has starting to have episodes of coughing and wheezing. Many infants and toddlers have colds and coughs but Michael has coughs without a runny nose. Every few days he has a severe episode of wheezing. The sharp sound of expelled air hitting his vocal cords is followed by a prolonged harsh, though musical noise. He has to fight to get the air out of his lungs so that he can take another breath in. His facial expression is one of strain and tension as he fights the narrowing of his airways. His chest bulges and the sterno-mastoid muscles at the sides of his neck stand out like cords. Again, Florrie and Manny are worried and fearful for their baby. Florrie asked Rachel what she should do. Rachel, anxious herself, tried to comfort her daughter with her presence at Michael's bedside. But she had never seen a child wheezing like that. They gave him cough mixtures. They asked the woman next door who told them to buy a brown liquid called Friar's Balsam that could be used to medicate the steam from boiling water which they should let Michael inhale with a towel over his head. When the next attack struck, they followed instructions with trembling hands but Michael hated having his head covered. He fought the towel and then turned his head away from the clouds of vapour, coughing and wheezing and hoarsely crying. They thought he was going to die. Eventually, the attack subsided and the wan, exhausted child lay recuperating in his mother's arms. But the following night he woke crying, and started wheezing again. They telephoned for Dr Samuel but were told he was already out on a call. Manny took the address (not far away) and went out to find him before he went home again. The month was May, but it was cold and wet and, of course, dark apart from a few streetlights. Nobody was about. He found the doctor just as he was emerging from his previous patient's front door. This would be his third call of the night and he was properly awake, though craving for a cup of tea. Manny spluttered out the symptoms and the doctor nodded, knowingly. Another kid with asthma. Thank God, he had some adrenaline and a clean syringe. He opened the passenger door of his Morris 12 and offered Manny a seat. They drove the short distance to number 6 Grange Crescent, in the darkness and the thin cold rain, with the wiper squeaking away.

In the house, at the bedside, Dr Samuel surveyed his tense struggling little patient with a fatherly compassion. He had children of his own. Thirty years later, one of his sons would endow a prize at Leeds Grammar School for the most promising pupil intending to study medicine. (I was the first winner.) He was a good old-fashioned family doctor who knew his patients and accepted that getting up at night was part of the job. He listened to Michael's chest with his long-tubed stethoscope and heard the continuous sounds that the textbooks call 'rhonchi'. He got his glass syringe and needle out from its case and placed it in the pan of boiling water that Florrie had provided. When it was sterilised and cool he drew up some adrenaline solution from a little bottle and injected it under the skin of Michael's forearm while his father held him firmly and his mother tried to soothe him. The treatment would be thought old-fashioned and dangerous nowadays but, thankfully, it worked. In less than a minute, Michael's tense facial muscles relaxed, his chest stopped heaving so painfully and the cracked organ music was replaced by normal breathing sounds.

Why does he get this asthma, they wanted to know. Is it something in the air? Are we giving him the wrong food? Privately, Dr Samuel subscribed to the theory that asthma was psychologically induced, the result of over-anxious parenting. But he was too wise to start expounding that in the middle of the night to two weary parents who already wondered if they were somehow to blame. So he told them it was a common complaint, probably due to the excessive smoke in the air and the prevailing dampness; and that certain foods might aggravate it. He did add that calm and quiet would help Michael to complete his recovery. And he prescribed some medicines. When he was a little older, but still getting attacks, Michael would have an atomiser which would spray a fine mist of bronchiole-relaxing medication into his lungs and relieve the attack nearly as quickly as the injection. It had a red rubber bulb attached by rubber tubing to a little glass bottle of medication, from the top of which the spray passed down a long fine metal tube to a nozzle that the patient put into his gaping mouth while he squeezed and inhaled. These were the antecedents of the little blue inhalers that asthma patients use nowadays. And of course there are now steroids and all sorts of other pharmacological products that have eased their lives and enriched the drug manufacturers. Nevertheless, children and adults still die from this strange episodic illness. I was familiar with inhalers as a child, because I too had attacks of asthma, though never as badly as Michael. And the first treatment I had was the atomiser.

In time, Florrie became accustomed to dealing with Michael's asthmatic crises. After a while she and Manny knew what to do. They would sit him up in bed with a pillow to hold on to and get him to use the atomiser which became a friendly comforter, to be kept in his cot in case of need. Grandma Rachel would come round and add her calming presence. If he didn't settle they would telephone for the doctor with his injection.

But ever since Michael started to be ill, Florrie has felt weighed down. A sense of foreboding grips her. Something terrible will happen. One day he will have an attack and not recover. She feels she has let him down in some indefinable way. She has let everyone down. She failed as a student. She has married a man who was unable to keep them secure until her father took over, to her shame and humiliation. And now she is failing as a mother. Her little boy was gasping for his life and she was powerless to save him. She slept badly and when she did she was haunted by dreams of children's coffins. During the day she tried to keep the bad thoughts away by concentrating on the housework. She cleaned the kitchen surfaces several times over. She made the bed with scrupulous care so there were no creases in the sheets and the pillows were symmetrically placed. If it wasn't quite right she would do it again. She swept the carpets and cleaned the floors. She polished the cutlery several times, always finding a spot of tarnish. Like Lady Macbeth. Psychiatrists call this kind of behaviour obsessive-compulsive. Some people are more neat and tidy than others but if taken to extremes it becomes a symptom if illness.

Manny has noticed the change in his wife's mood and behaviour and he is worried. He likes to come home to a clean and tidy house, but this is going too far. And she has such a strained look on her face, so grim and careworn. It's hard to get her to smile anymore. And sometimes she cries to herself beside him at night, and can't or won't be comforted.

Why are you doing this, Florrie, I want to ask her. Once more, I try to merge with her, to thread my way into her thoughts. From in here the world seems small and distant, now. She feels numb and detached. She is aware of Manny and her mother, reaching out their hands, trying to pull her back to them. She watches their efforts dispassionately as if through soundproof glass. I feel as though I am acting a part in play, she thinks. I could break out of this if I wanted and let them talk to me. But something in me says no, stay here, don't let them reach you. Nothing there for you now.

Manny and Rachel have a conference. He can talk to her in a way that isn't possible with his father-in-law. They are both desperately worried. What can have happened to their lovely girl? They call in Dr Samuel, who is kind and he listens. He is psychologically aware, as we know; the little boy has psychosomatic illnesses, he reflects, and now the mother is depressed. She's had a worrying time. The husband seems a good sort. They've had money troubles but so have most people. Maybe I should ask her a bit more about herself. She's a bright girl, started at the university but then she failed an exam and her father wouldn't let her continue. I should stay and talk to her but I've got three more calls to do before evening surgery. 'Canst thou not minister to a mind diseas'd?' he asks himself, remembering Macbeth's peevish question to the family doctor about his wife's condition. 'Therein the patient must minister to himself' was the doctor's reply. Not very helpful, but what can you do? He prescribes a female tonic, a sedative and plenty of rest. He says that Florrie should leave the housework to the maid, even if it's not done so well without her supervision. He will call again and see how she is progressing.

But she doesn't progress. Rachel talks to her sister-in-law, Annie. You may remember that she is the wife of Jacob's brother Isaac who helped him and Rachel when they first came to Leeds. Their son, Cousin Henry, is now a family doctor in London. When Henry and Dolly, his wife, come to Leeds for a weekend visit, they see Florrie and are shocked by the way she sits and doesn't smile and replies in monosyllables if at all. They feel uncomfortable and are relieved when Florrie goes upstairs to see to Michael. The others have a conference in the kitchen. Cousin Henry has plenty of Rostov drive and decisiveness. He has made a diagnosis and he has a plan of action.

Listen, he says, Florrie is having a nervous breakdown. It's probably because of the strain of the pregnancy and the confinement and then Michael being so ill. She needs medical treatment.

She has seen Dr Samuel says Manny. He gave her this medicine.

Henry looks at the bottle and waves it away.

That won't help. Samuel is not a bad doctor in his way but he is out of his depth here. Florrie needs to see a nerve specialist in London.

What kind of treatment should she have? asks Rachel.

There are new ideas about these disorders now. All based on talking to the patient and analysing the subconscious mind. They may use hypnosis. It all started with this man Freud in Vienna, one of our people. Julia knows all about it, and she personally knows a specialist who uses the method. What I propose is that Florrie comes to stay with Dolly and me in London, say for a month. Julia will introduce her to the specialist and the treatment can begin.

Dolly nods in agreement.

But what about Michael, asks Manny? Can she take him too?

Michael will stay here with me, says Rachel firmly.

Manny feels that everything is spinning out of control. He is afraid of losing both his wife and his little son to these powerful Rostovs. But perhaps they know best. And he has nothing else to suggest.

When they put the plan to Florrie she looks blankly at them and says, what about Michael? When Rachel repeats her offer, she nods and says all right. I'll go but only for a week or two.

Henry knows it will take longer than that but decides it's prudent to say no more at this stage. Rachel helps her to pack her suitcases and a few days later, Henry and Dolly collect her in a taxi and take her to the station. Little Michael waves uncertainly from the safety of his grandmother's arms. Manny stands on the doorstep, feeling a sense of relief that his wife is going to be restored to health and when she returns she will love him again as she did before things started to go wrong. It seems a long time ago.

Chapter 9
On the couch

So Florrie travels to London on the same train that her father uses to go to the bristle auctions. She watches the scenery flash by but she doesn't really see anything. She is thinking, is this the end of my life? Will I ever see Michael and Manny and my parents again? Perhaps it's for the best. I am no use to anyone like this. Nothing gives me pleasure. I don't want to eat, I can't listen to music any more, I feel so empty. And she cries silently as the train rattles along. Henry and Dolly look at her with concern and Dolly takes her hand, which is slightly comforting. When they get to their destination, she is numb to the noise and bustle of the capital. She scarcely takes in the details of her cousins' house about which she had always been intensely curious. It should be exciting to see it and to live in, but it isn't. She registers that it's a corner house in a quiet street. They usher her in and show her to her room. Later Henry shows her his consulting room and the two waiting rooms, one for panel patients, the other, carpeted, for the more well-to-do private customers. She nods and tries to look interested. She is glad to escape to her bedroom where sleep eventually overcomes her; it has been a long day.

When the day of the first appointment arrives. Florrie is taken by taxi, with Henry as her escort, from Willesden, down the Edgware Road and then Marylebone Road to the medical heartland of Welbeck Street where, at number 12, Dr Eder has his rooms.

Henry rings the bell and Florrie is admitted by a maid, or possibly a nurse, in a frilly cap. She is directed to the waiting room and given the illustrated papers. Henry takes his leave, tells his cousin she will be fine, Dr Eder is very nice and says he will return to collect her in an hour.

Who is this Dr Eder to whom her family have entrusted Florrie's fragile soul?

He was the son of a diamond merchant (one of our people) born in London in 1866, which makes him 59 when Florrie first met him and just 10 years older than her father. He had studied medicine and qualified in 1895 after several failed attempts. So, like Florrie, he had not found it easy, but, unlike her, he had persevered. As a young man he had had many intellectual interests and had found it hard to settle down. He travelled in South Africa and South America; he had been active in left wing politics and saw himself as a socialist; he had looked after the health of poor Londoners in charitable clinics in Deptford and Bow. Then he developed a passionate interest in psychoanalysis, read all he could about it and had some personal analysis with Ernest Jones who was Freud's most distinguished disciple in London. In 1913, Eder travelled to Vienna and got to know Freud personally. During the war he treated shell-shocked soldiers in Malta and in London. Then in 1918 his interest switched to the Homeland Organisation and its efforts to settle our people in Palestine. He spent several years in Jerusalem as a member of the Homeland Commission. In 1923 we see his interest returning to psychoanalysis. He wanted to have more personal analysis with Freud, but the Master was too busy. Undeterred, Dr Eder took himself to Budapest and had eight months treatment with Freud's favourite pupil, Sandor Ferenczi. As historians of psychoanalysis will tell us, Ferenczi was a very different character from Freud, warm-hearted and outgoing with his patients, when Freud, perhaps due to the constant pain from his jaw cancer, was becoming increasingly austere. Some would accuse Ferenczi of being too familiar with his patients and allowing them to cross the strict professional boundary. He upset Freud by telling him in a letter that he had hugged, or even kissed a patient. Whether this happened more than once, we don't know. But Ferenczi certainly allowed himself to be moved by the suffering of his patients and wanted to treat them as human beings rather than objects of scientific study. Was Dr Eder's approach influenced by this distinguished if slightly unorthodox analyst? We shall see.

Florrie sits in another waiting room until, at exactly 10 a.m., the door opens and Dr Eder greets her. He is a stockily built man of medium height with greying hair, receding at the temples. He has a firmly modelled nose and a bristling moustache. His eyes are kindly with a twinkle. She is struck by his resemblance to her father!

Good morning, Mrs Levinsky, please follow me.

Florrie obediently follows the comfortably solid doctor into his oak-panelled consulting room. It contains a large desk and chair for the doctor and a chair for the patient, which he invites her to occupy. On the other side of the room she notices a leather couch covered with a soft blanket. She knows about the couch from Dolly's sister Julia (the doctor) who has briefed her about what to expect. (You'll go every day, Florrie, and lie on the couch and just say everything that comes into your head. What if nothing comes? Don't worry, it will.) After a short speech of introduction and asking her if she has any questions, which she hasn't, she is indeed invited to lie down and be a patient.

It seems an odd thing to do at first, but the couch is quite comfortable and she can no longer see the doctor because he has moved his chair to a position just behind her head. He asks her a few questions about her family of origin, her marriage and her little boy. Then it starts properly. I want you just to tell me anything that comes into your head. It doesn't have to make sense. It will seem strange at first but you will find it gets easier.

Florrie starts to tell him, slowly, about Michael and his illnesses. He leads her on to talk about her own childhood. She describes her parents. Then how she feels she has disappointed them. Emotion wells up in her. I can feel the constriction in her throat. Then she can't control it any more, and he says to let go and a huge sob escapes her. She starts to cry and now she can't stop. She breathes in great heaving sighs, the tears pour from her hot, red eyes, and she fumbles for a handkerchief. Dr Eder silently supplies one. He murmurs encouragingly. He is so nice. She wishes he would bend down and gather her in his arms so she can cry on his shoulder. She wishes she could sit on his knee. Dr Eder is intuitively aware of this and the thought flashes into his mind that he would like to grant her unspoken wish, because she is a lovely girl and he is touched deeply by her unhappiness. But he restrains himself, remembering the advice of Professor Ferenczi in Budapest. There will be times, the kindly little professor had said, when you will want to hold and even kiss the patient especially the female patient, become her protector, even her lover. And love is probably what she needs. But we

70

mustn't get involved like that. She has her own life and we have ours. So we must hold back a little, David! Hold back. But be generous with your love, don't be stern, like a severe father. Him, your patient has already.

So Dr Eder remains impassive, although sympathy flows from him in gentle waves. Florrie cries and wipes her eyes, blows her nose on the doctor's handkerchief and cries again. It seems to her and to me that the crying will never end. Then Dr Eder says quietly, it's time to stop now. I shall see you again at the same time tomorrow.

As she turns at the door to say goodbye, he looks into her wet eyes and is flooded by an overwhelming feeling of loss.

On the next day, Tuesday, she cries again, but not so much. She is able to tell him about her childhood and her life at home with her brothers. How she both loves and hates them; which Dr Eder says is quite normal. How she enjoyed her schooldays; being top of the class and praised by her teachers who predicted great achievements. Her exhilarating year at the University and how it ended in bewilderment and humiliation. On Wednesday, she tells him about Manny and he asks about their sex life. She was expecting this because Julia had warned her that this was what analysts did and there was no need for a modern woman to be shocked; but all the same it seemed rather improper. She loved Manny, she told him, and had always felt good when he made love to her. He seemed satisfied. Then she came to the financial crisis and the shame she felt because Manny couldn't give her security, and her father had to rescue them. She cried again when she told him how her father and her brothers had criticised him and practically accused him of marrying her under false pretences. When she got up from the couch and thanked him at the end of that session, she felt better. She could even smile at the doctor and he smiled back. He is a good man, she thought. He is so interested in all the details and he seems to understand what I'm going through.

On Thursday he disturbed her by telling her that little girls fell in love with their fathers before they even met their husbands. She had almost certainly had *sexual* feelings about her father, although they had been repressed into her unconscious mind so she wouldn't remember. But they were aroused by the conflict in her mind between loyalty to her husband and to her father who seemed so much stronger. She didn't know what to say about this, and there was an uncomfortable silence. It was absurd, how could she feel like that about Dad – and what about Mother? Confusion and embarrassment. Silence. After a while Dr Eder asked her how she slept. She could only sleep, she said if she took the green medicine that Dr Samuel had prescribed. Did she have any dreams? Yes, but she couldn't remember them. Get a notebook and write them down, advised the doctor, before you forget. Your unconscious will speak to us through your dreams. I will see you again tomorrow.

That night she had a dream and, in the morning, she wrote down as much as she could remember in her notebook.

On Friday, she lies on the couch and Dr Eder says well, Florrie, did you have any dreams? Florrie says yes I did, feeling pleased that she is able to produce her homework. And she tells him the dream.

Florrie's dream
She is walking round the big lake in Roundhay Park with Jimmy Barclay, her old sweetheart. There is a small animal in the water, perhaps a lamb. It struggles and appears to be drowning. Jimmy jumps in and tries to rescue it but he disappears under the water. The little animal continues to struggle. Her parents appear. Her father has a long fishing rod, which he tells her was very expensive. He says it's time to go home now and her mother takes her hand, saying how cold it is. She realises she has lost a glove but doesn't want to tell her mother. She feels very ashamed.

Dr Eder doesn't say whether he is pleased with the dream or not. He explains the free association method of dream analysis. He breaks the dream up into segments like a geneticist dividing up the DNA on a chromosome.

Start with the lake.

Oh, says Florrie, it's a big lake in the park in Leeds. It's actually called The Big Lake, or sometimes the Waterloo Lake. We used to all go for a walk there every Sunday with my parents and brothers. Now my parents take me and Michael on Saturday afternoons.

What about your husband?

Manny can't come because he works all day on Saturday. That's when he gets most of his customers.

Tell me about Jimmy Barclay.

Oh, he was just somebody I got to know on holiday in the country once. When I was about 13. I was – very fond of him. He liked me too. He was 16. I thought I wanted to marry him.

What was he like?

He was a very sweet boy.

Do you still think about him sometimes?

Yes I do.

Her voice breaks a little and Dr Eder wonders if she is going to cry.

He gave me, he gave me, I still have a little gold heart that he gave me as a keepsake. I knew I wouldn't see him again. My parents wouldn't have approved if it had got serious. I mean they liked him but he wasn't – one of our people – so it wouldn't have worked.

Dr Eder softens. He often sees young women in distress on his couch, but he is always moved and sometimes, as with Florrie, a little stirred. Now she is crying softly and again he offers the handkerchief from his breast pocket which is gratefully received.

When he sees that she has recovered he asks gently, what about the little lamb? What does that make you think of?

Florrie remembers the lambs on the farm where she met Jimmy Barclay. He was always very good with them. Some had lost their mother and had to be hand-fed. She didn't remember any of them falling into a lake although the bigger sheep were dipped.

What about your little lamb, asks Dr Eder archly. Your little Michael.

We are always very careful not to let him fall in the lake.

I am thinking, says the doctor, that when he has an asthma attack, he is gasping for breath just like a little lamb that is drowning.

And he thinks to himself, how useful it is to be medically trained and to know what a child with asthma looks like. Florrie looks suddenly alert. She has taken that one in, he can see. She gets it. She knows that little lamb is human now. But Florrie herself is a lost lamb as well. His thoughts race ahead. Perhaps Jimmy Barclay would have been a better shepherd than the man she married. He decides not to say that just now.

The Professor always advised, don't say too much. Even if you are right, David, it may be the wrong time to say it.

Does that struggling in the water make you think of anything else?

Not really. I've always been a good swimmer.

Sometimes, when one is very anxious it can feel like drowning. As if you will die and no one will save you.

I have been anxious, doctor. I told you about our money troubles and the way my family treated my husband...

And part of you thought, yes they are right. He is not strong enough to pull you out of the water. He will just go under.

I don't know. Perhaps a little.

And that thought made you ashamed, I think

Silence.

(Don't go too fast, David! Stay only one step ahead of your patient)

Let's go on to your parents. When you think of them appearing in the dream, what comes into your mind? Does your father like fishing?

No, he has never fished. Isn't that strange? But my brother Harry loves fishing. I've been out with him sometimes, but it's very boring just sitting and freezing on the river bank.

Does he ever catch anything?

Oh yes, but that's even worse. It's disgusting to see them struggling for air when he takes them off the hook and lays them on the ground to die.

In the dream your father says the fishing rod is expensive.

Well if he did go fishing he would want to have only the best.

And she goes on talking about her parents and how they value nice things and respect people who have plenty of money. It's because they had to struggle so hard when they first came to England as poor immigrants. She gets quite animated and is surprised and slightly miffed when Dr Eder calls 'time' and seems abruptly to switch himself off. They haven't even finished the dream.

The weekend is surprisingly difficult. She has got used to the routine of going down to Welbeck Street in a taxi and talking to the friendly doctor as she lies on his couch. Then on Friday he seemed to change. Why was he so curt and cold at the end? He seemed to lose interest in her completely just because the time was up. Perhaps he had another patient waiting. She immediately felt a surge of jealousy for the unknown rival, probably another girl, lying on the couch still warm from her own body. Perhaps crying and using the doctor's handkerchief. She hoped it was a clean one; and the thought of the other girl having to use the same one made her laugh and think, this is ridiculous.

But all through Saturday and Sunday, Doctor Eder was in her mind. He had seemed such a friend, so kind and gentle and he understood her perfectly. But then came the change and the coldness. Was she always going to be let down by people she loved? She was a little shocked at the idea of loving the doctor (she didn't love Dr Samuel, kind and reassuring though he always was). She didn't mention any of this to her cousins, Henry and Dolly. But they both noticed at dinnertime that she was a little more lively and even laughed at one of Henry's jokes. On Sunday, Julia came to visit and offered to take her to the pictures. After a little hesitation, Florrie agreed. They took a red bus to the West End and saw *The Black Pirate* with Douglas Fairbanks in two-tone Technicolor. After the film they had tea in a café and Julia asked how the treatment was going. Did she like Dr Eder?

Oh yes, he's very kind. Except...

Except what? I don't know. Are you missing him?

Florrie coloured and Julia squeezed her hand.

That always happens. It's called transference and it's part of the treatment. You transfer feelings to him that belong to other people in your life like your parents. It's not a real feeling and it will go away as he interprets it for you. I'll lend you a book, it's actually by Dr Eder's sister-in-law, that explains it all very simply.

But Florrie thought: suppose the feeling is real and it won't go away?

On Monday, she is confident enough to take two buses to Welbeck Street by herself. She is wearing a smart new red coat and a cloche hat. She has put on her makeup carefully and her lipstick matches the coat. She wonders what he will be like after the weekend. Has he thought about her at all? She wonders if he and his wife went see the same picture at the weekend. Again a pang of jealousy hits her as she rings the bell and the maid lets her in.

The weekends are always difficult, says Dr Eder.

He is kind and understanding again now, but the Friday dismissal still rankles.

And you will find the holidays even worse. When we talk like this you begin to see me as if I were your father or even your mother. (Dr Eder! You're not a bit like my mother. You have a moustache!) Well yes, I think I am, in spite of my moustache, because when you lie on the couch and tell me your troubles your child self remembers how both your parents looked after you and were kind to you as a little one.

But I'm not a child any more.

My dear, we all have a part of ourselves that remains a child as long as we live. (He called me his dear!) Your mother and father love you and care for you, but when it's bed time you have to let them leave you for a while to live their grown up life. And that separation can be very painful. Like your weekend away from me.

You never even finished my dream. (I am so cheeky with him! I feel I have always known him.)

That's true. Have you had any more thoughts about it?

And he thinks: the transference has taken hold. She accepts me. And she is so cheeky today. But I think she felt real pain. She is so sweet. I must be careful. I must concentrate.

And so Florrie talks about the last part of the dream, where her parents want to take her home but she feels cold and has lost a glove about which she feels ashamed.

The doctor starts to explain what it means. He reminds her about her parents looking after her jointly: hand in glove. He keeps harping back to the Friday feeling (as he calls it) and how she felt he had 'gone cold' on her. He says that the word 'glove' is 'love' with a 'g' at the beginning, so it's as if she has lost some love and feels ashamed about that.

This seems too far-fetched to Florrie. How can he be so sure about these crazy ideas? They have a bit of an argument which is closed by Dr Eder saying 'it's time'. She is furious with him for winning the argument like that. But when she gets up from the couch and turns to face him, he smiles and she forgives him.

More weeks go by and Florrie continues to attend from Monday to Friday. The dream soon becomes a regular theme. Other dreams follow but they all seem to lead back to the same ideas, at least where the doctor is concerned. He interprets cautiously, sensitive to what she will accept. Naturally her father would have a more expensive fishing rod than her husband could afford (supposing he wanted one). Privately Dr Eder notes that it's a phallic symbol as well but he decides not to point that out at this stage. They move on to Florrie's repetitive behaviour, her washing, cleaning and tidying. She concedes that she might be too much of a perfectionist. Her mother taught her how to fold sheets carefully and she used to think it was stupid. Now she can't bear it if the creases don't fall in the right places and she has to start again. Whoever is helping her at the other end of the sheet has to be very patient.

Dr Eder thinks she is trying to restore a perfect world where there are no creases and everything is clean. He suspects that her unconscious anger seems to have caused all the mess and the dirt and the crumpled hopes in her inner world. She listens but is not convinced. Does it matter?

Their relationship continues to deepen. He develops respect for his patient as well as parental love with just a tinge of the erotic, well under control. And Florrie? She is engrossed and possessed by the whole experience. She feels that Dr Eder knows her and cares for her in a special way, even if she doesn't agree with all his ideas about her. He doesn't mind what she says or how much she cries. She is definitely feeling more alive. But she misses Michael and Manny, especially at the weekends.

Chapter 10
Coming home

Florrie had now been in London for three months. During that time she had been home four times. It distressed her that Michael seemed at first to prefer his grandma's arms to her own. Gradually, over the weekend, he would warm to her again and walk around holding her hand. But then she had to leave again and, sensing the change, he would go back to Rachel. Florrie wanted to stay before she lost him completely. But she also wanted to go back to Dr Eder and continue the treatment with him. Manny reassured her and urged her to continue until she was 'completely better'. She wanted to say that it wasn't like a medical cure; it was more like a growing relationship, a gradual revelation, a journey of self-discovery, an adventure. She didn't think he would understand that, so it was better for them all to think of it as a cure.

Fortunately, Michael had had only a few mild asthma attacks and the family had coped without having to call the doctor. But how long should she go on? Back in London after three months of analysis, she asked Henry and Dolly what they thought. Dolly sympathised with her separation from Michael. Henry said that the treatment often went on for months, even years in some cases. Some of the analysts dragged it out deliberately, in his opinion, for the sake of the fees, but Eder was a sound chap who wouldn't do that. They consulted Julia who said that Florrie ought to discuss it with Dr Eder.

Well, that sounds a good idea. He must have known that there was a serious conflict for her between her relationship with the doctor and her separation from her baby son. I find myself thinking about Anna Karenina having to choose between her little son and her lover. Of course, Dr Eder is no Vronsky, but these events remind me of Tuesday afternoons, when as a small boy I was given my tea and entertained by my father because Florrie was away keeping a mysterious appointment. Later I realised that she was seeing another analyst. No wonder that, in my first reading of *Anna Karenina*, I tended to identify with little Seriozha. Why couldn't Florrie just fetch Michael to London with her? Couldn't Henry and Dolly have looked after him? Dolly was now studying dentistry in London and besides she had no experience yet of children of her own. On the other hand, Florrie's analysis only took up about 90 minutes a day including travelling, so they might have found a baby sitter.

Dr Eder was unprepared for the question of 'how much longer?' In his enjoyment of the analysis, he had tended to forget about Florrie's little lamb and to be reminded of this negligence gave him some discomfort. Had counter-transference carried him away? She hadn't raised it before, and women tended to find other women to look after their children without too much difficulty. The child was with his grandmother, he would be fine. He and his wife had been unable to have children so the problem had never occurred. Then he tried out the idea of his child self being separated from his own mother – and didn't care for it. In the end he proposed that they go on for another month and then there would be a holiday break for three weeks. After that, Florrie could come back for a few more weeks and decide whether she wanted (or needed) to go on.

Dr Eder's holiday was a bit of a blow for Florrie. She didn't see why he couldn't just stay in London while she had a holiday with Michael. He reminded her gently of her transference jealousy of his private life. And so she went back to Leeds and her family for three weeks in which she didn't suffer jealousy and felt much better. She was able to look after Michael; to play with him every day and feel more like his real mother, rather than a visitor from the past. She still did too much housework too many times over and made Manny help her fold the sheets more than once until she was satisfied. But she smiled and talked again and he was relieved to find her happier.

What was the treatment like? he asked her. Did he ask about your childhood? Did you tell him your dreams?

Manny had been reading the book on Florrie's bedside table. It was called *The Unconscious in Action* and it was by Dr Eder's sister-in-law, another analyst, called Barbara Low. My Dad was a great reader who made up for having to leave school at 14 by finding things out for himself. I think I take after him in that way, preferring my own researches to attending lectures.

I just lie on the couch and talk (she said). Yes I do tell him my dreams and they sort of lead on to other things. He's very kind. And he understands how I feel.

Manny feels a sharp little dart of jealousy. Don't I understand you? I do my best.

I know you do. But this is different. I can't really explain it.

Do you talk about me?

Florrie smiles. Not very much! It's more about the past. And about – how I feel. She doesn't really want to tell him how the doctor makes her feel. He says it's all 'transference' but she is not always sure she agrees.

Do you want to go back?

Yes. I think we have more work to do. I hate leaving you and Michael. But there are things about myself I still have to sort out.

Manny accepts her decision although he feels excluded from the mysterious world of London and psychoanalysis. Anything is better than seeing Florrie so withdrawn and miserable. And of course her father is paying for the treatment. Manny doesn't even know how much it costs. He puts on his overcoat and his trilby hat; picks up his brown paper parcel, tucks it under his arm, shuts the door behind him and walks to the bus stop. He too has his work to do, earning what he can.

So, in the New Year (1927) she returns to London and resumes her sessions with Dr Eder. There are more dreams, more recollections of childhood, more thoughts about her father. And more complex, sometimes painful emotions circling round the man who sits behind her head, listening and commenting, remembering everything she tells him. He gives her all his attention and his love. But only till the session ends and then she has to go out into the street and someone else takes her place. Until the same time the next day. Sometimes she reproaches and scolds him. He can still make her cry. Sometimes she sees the funny side and they have a joke together. She reads more books about psychoanalysis including one by Freud himself. Henry and Dolly don't ask her about the treatment but they can see she is more relaxed. By the spring, Dr Eder is talking about the sessions coming to an end. They will have to say goodbye. It will remind her of other partings, other losses. But something good will remain, he hopes, to sustain her. Florrie wishes she could go on forever. Wishes she could marry Dr Eder or be his little girl. But she also knows that she has another life in Leeds with Manny and she owes it to Michael to be there as his mother.

Back in Leeds she slipped easily into her old life of being with Michael, shopping, cooking, cleaning the house. When her tasks were done she could visit her mother and the two of them might take Michael for a walk, using the little pushcart when he was tired. In the evening she would put Michael to bed and get supper ready for when Manny came home, which was not till 7 o'clock because of his full day in Dewsbury and the double bus ride to get home.

At the weekends she would see her friends who were mainly single women whose fiancés and boyfriends had never returned from the war. There were the three White sisters who helped their father to run the Cottage Road cinema; there were also the Sclare sisters, May, Rose and Pearl with whom she played bridge. May was big and hearty with a broad laugh; Rose was thin and precise and studying to be a dentist; Pearl stayed home and kept house for them after their mother died. And of course, there was Ray, a vigorous, demonstrative girl with tight corkscrew curls who worked at the Ministry of Labour. They all liked Manny whose status with them was much higher than with his three brothers-in-law. He stayed in the background during the bridge games, occasionally offering advice, but rarely taking a hand himself. Sometimes he would just sit in the kitchen and read, smoking a cigarette and joining them for a cup of tea.

Did Florrie miss Dr Eder? Did it feel like being parted from her lover? There was a nostalgic ache from time to time; especially in the first few weeks, between 10 am when her sessions started, and ten minutes to eleven, when they finished. But it gradually faded as she became more engaged with life in Leeds. By the summer she knew that she was pregnant again.

Chapter 11
Mother of two

On April 16th 1928 Florrie gave birth, in the front bedroom to a second baby boy. He came easily, with the midwife in attendance and a brief visit from Dr Friend who was Dr Samuel's colleague. The new baby was perfectly fit with dark brown hair and brown eyes, in contrast to his fair-haired, blue-eyed brother. He was named Kenneth, but not given a middle name. To Florrie and Manny's great relief, he was sturdy and healthy and never suffered from the asthma and eczema that continued to plague Michael at intervals.

The next few years were peaceful ones for Florrie. Her life was centred on her two little ones and there was no need to worry too much what her life was all about or where it was going. There was another sickening downward lurch in the economy in 1929, with a stock market crash in London echoing the larger one in New York. But Florrie and Manny were hardly affected. People continued to listen to Wigfalls' radios and to ride the bicycles that they also sold. Manny continued to get commissions for a few suits and some fur coats. One year passed into another. The children grew bigger and developed into a pair of little boys who were companionable and a delight to their parents, the only anxiety being Michael's recurrent attacks of asthma. Florrie's depression had lifted. Her washing and cleaning compulsions had receded. Now and then her thoughts turned to Dr Eder and she wondered how he was getting on and who was now lying on his couch in Welbeck Street. But on the whole she was content to be part of the rhythm of life in Leeds. She had her own little family and she was still very close to her parents and her brothers.

Every Saturday, Jacob Rostov (Grandpa Rostov as I think of him) would go to the synagogue with his younger sons, Abe and Benny. His eldest son, Harry, had stopped going in his teens, saying he didn't believe in God any more and preferred to go fishing. Florrie didn't find this particularly shocking because she wasn't sure that she believed in God either. When I asked her, one day, if she believed in Him, she replied that she believed we should all be good and kind to each other. I concluded from this that, though a moral person, she did not believe in a higher power and that therefore there was no need for me to believe either. (This did not prevent me from addressing fervent requests and promises of good behaviour to the non-existent deity at times of stress.) My two younger uncles may have been more religious or were just less inclined to rebel. All three of them were able to recite the services in the ancient language of our faith. Harry was the most fluent.

Florrie would go round to her parents' house with the two children later in the morning to help her mother to get the dinner ready. Meanwhile Manny would have left the house early, with his parcel under his arm, to catch the bus to town, followed by the bus to Dewsbury. There, in the upstairs part of the shop, he would sit and wait for customers. After the service, Jacob and his sons would return to Mexborough Drive and assemble round the dinner table. I am thinking now of a time before Florrie's brothers were married and were still living with their parents. Michael is six and Kenneth is three. There is an appetising smell of good homeland food. They will have chopped liver and onion, followed by chicken noodle soup, then chicken breast with roast potatoes and carrots. For dessert there might be a *lokshen* pudding made from noodles baked with cinnamon and currants. There will be glasses of sparkling 'Tizer' for the children. After the meal, Harry, Abe and Benny take turns to entertain their nephews. The little boys are fond of their three uncles, and Florrie likes to see them playing together. Harry tends to get them over-excited, showing them tricks and staging elaborate games that involve running round the house and the garden. This makes Florrie a little uneasy. One of them might fall onto the rockery and get hurt. And all that laughing might bring on Michael's asthma. Abe with his limp can't join in these games; but he asks Michael about school and tells them both stories; sometimes he will sit at the piano (where his movements are suddenly smooth and assured) and sing them comic songs. Florrie watches and feels a glow of pleasure. She also wonders how much pain Abe is in from his hip and his deformed leg, and how hard it is to conceal it. When it is Benny's turn, he likes to take photographs of them; then take them to watch the pictures emerging like ghosts in the mysterious darkroom with its red light bulb. Round about five o' clock, Florrie and the boys return home.

At seven o'clock, their father will come through the door, with his parcel, smiling and enjoying reunion with his family. He was always excluded by circumstances from the Rostov family Saturdays. Maybe he felt a little hurt that the Rostov boys could play with his children while he was exiled in Dewsbury. But he was never quite at ease with his in-laws and perhaps it was better to be in Dewsbury.

When Florrie told him about her parents' new furniture and Jacob's new car he marvelled at the continuing success of their business. How did this trade in bristles manage to support a family of five adults in such prosperity in such difficult times? He found it hard to understand. Jacob had by now acquired new premises in Manor Street, not far from home. The building had enough space for an office, a warehouse and a workshop where the newly imported bristles could be processed and repackaged for sale to customers. Jacob's plan had always been for his sons to join him and ultimately to inherit the business. Florrie was aware that this caused a good deal of rumbling discontent. She knew that Harry had been top of his class in every subject at school and should have gone to university. When Jacob told him this was out of the question there was an angry scene followed by prolonged sulking from Harry and a stiff determination from Jacob. He knew that Harry would be unable to find a way of paying the fees and would have to give in. Florrie was sorry for her brother but it was no good arguing with Dad. In the end, Harry decided to apply his energy and his ideas to the business and to enjoy himself with his friends in his spare time. He and Benny were the travellers, taking it in turns to drive round the brush makers of Yorkshire and Lancashire looking for renewal of their orders. And going down to London for the auctions. Abe, being lame and unable to drive, was given the job of bookkeeper and accountant as well as dealing with correspondence. He would sit in the little office, perched on a high stool, leaning on an even higher desk and writing in a huge leather bound ledger. On her rare trips to Manor Street, Florrie would see him scratching away with his pen and be reminded of Bob Cratchitt or some other Dickensian clerk. Yet Abe, whose expectations were lower than his brothers', seemed quite content with his role in the business. And the arrival of an assistant, in the shape of a secretary, was to make him even happier. But we will come to that in due course.

Benny was the only one who made a serious bid to escape from the bristle house.

One afternoon, he came round to see Florrie while Manny was at work. He was now 21, slim, good looking and well dressed, with a neat little moustache.

Flo, I've got something to tell you. (Flo was his special name for her) I can't tell Ma and Dad just yet, but I want you to know. Can you keep it dark?

It depends what it is. I hope you're not in trouble, Benny.

Benny scratches his head. I'm not in trouble. It's just that I can't bear the thought of working in Dad's warehouse and trying to flog bristles all my life. It's so boring. There are other things I want to do, that I could do. He is such a tyrant. We all did well at school; he should have let us go to the university. And he stopped you as soon as you had any difficulty. No, Benny, it wasn't like that. I didn't want to go on.

Well, anyway, he didn't let us boys go at all. So the thing is that I am leaving. I am getting out of here.

How can you do that? Where will you go?

Benny looks round conspiratorially to see if anyone is listening. But the children are playing in the yard. Then he smiles engagingly at his sister.

I'm going to be a journalist! I wrote to lots of papers and I've got a job on a paper in Lancashire. In a town called Ashton-under-Lyne. Yes really. It is a funny name. I had an interview there last week and they've offered me a job as a junior reporter. I'm leaving tomorrow.

But Benny, where will you live? Ma will be so worried. And Dad will be furious.

I know. But it's all right. I have some digs in Ashton. It's not as big as Leeds but it's not a bad little place. We have customers there so I visit quite often. I want you to reassure Ma that I'm all right. I'll leave them a letter and I'll phone them in a while.

But I am not coming back to fetch and carry Dad's bloody bristles, excuse my French, Flo.

What will Harry and Abe think?

Harry had his chance to walk out but he didn't. It's different for Abe. He likes it in the office. They'll get over it. And the business will just have to manage without me.

Florrie hasn't seen Benny quite like this before; she is used to thinking of him as the baby. It is quite exciting to see him all fired up, setting off bravely by himself on a big adventure. A small part of her wishes she was going with him. But she is also worried about how her parents will react. She tells Manny when he gets home, and he is intrigued but doesn't feel involved.

That night, she has difficulty sleeping. In the morning her mother is on the telephone. Benny has gone to Lancashire! He left a note! He has a job with a newspaper, he says. Her father is predictably annoyed. Florrie tries to be sympathetic. Strangely, they don't ask if he confided in his sister so she doesn't have to lie to them.

Benny enjoyed his time with the paper. He had a chance to use his talents and his ideas. Independence was good for him. But his freedom lasted only a few months. Before long Jacob and Harry came to Ashton several times to see him. First they argued, then they pleaded and finally they negotiated. Perhaps he was feeling homesick by then. Perhaps they offered him more money and greater responsibility. He was back in Leeds and back selling bristles by the end of the year.

As the decade wore on, the bristle business expanded and proved capable of supporting three more little families. Over the course of five years (1931-35) The Rostov brothers all got married and moved to houses of their own. Harry was first. He was a tall, strong-looking young man with an exciting outgoing manner and a wicked grin that appealed to the girls. When I see Clark Gable in an old movie I think: there's Uncle Harry. Florrie loved him and was proud of him; but she always had the slight anxiety that he was going to get out of control, do something dangerous. Suppose he got one of these girls 'into trouble'? He was so attractive, it could easily happen with one of the silly creatures who wrapped their arms round his neck and kissed him extravagantly. In the end, Harry was mesmerised by a tall, slim, wondrously beautiful girl from out of town called Stella. When she came along he lost interest in all the others. Florrie was pleased to see that he was settling down. She liked Stella although she realised that her own more terrestrial good looks were now eclipsed by Stella's film-star glamour. Harry and Stella had a daughter. But sadly, Stella was to die of leukaemia at the age of 34 when her little girl was only twelve. The graves in our cemetery in Leeds are arranged in straight lines in chronological order. When I walk along the line of memorial stones it is always a shock to see Auntie Stella buried with all the old people who died in the same year (1946) in their seventies or eighties. What is she doing there, with all those old folks, I wonder. It seems that she appeared in our world like a supernova and within a short dream-like space of time was gone. I have to remind myself that Harry and Stella did have 15 happy years together.

Meanwhile, as I hinted earlier, romance was also brightening Abe's life in his Dickensian office. Jacob and Harry decided that they needed a secretary who would type the letters, look after the filing, make the tea and generally assist Abe. They hired a lively, petite young girl with red hair and a voice that was sometimes high pitched and sometimes seductively low. Her name was Tess, and she and Abe got on well from the beginning. Always self-conscious about his small stature and awkward lurching gait, Abe had never tried very hard with girls. He observed the easy way in which his brothers introduced themselves to girls and made them laugh. They would look at his brothers admiringly, readily accept invitations to the pictures and soon be willing to hold hands and kiss. Abe was so afraid of rejection that he didn't even try. This shyness made the girls feel uneasy with him. He couldn't dance, and on the rare occasions when he went to a dance hall with the others he spent his time sitting at the bar. But now he had a pretty, vivacious girl keeping him company in the office every day and chatting away as if there were no barriers between them. He could make her laugh and she was not afraid to come close so that he could smell her perfume. Sometimes she would touch his arm or pat his shoulder. Going to the office became a pleasure. When Tess suggested they have a date at the pictures, his joy was complete. Now he had a girl to go out with like everyone else. She didn't mind walking slowly with him; she tucked her arm into his and couldn't care less about being seen hanging on to an awkward boy with a limp.

But Jacob, his father, and Harry, his elder brother observed the flowering of Abe and Tess's romance and were not pleased. They didn't mind the giggles and the intimacy in the office, which they couldn't help noticing when they passed through to consult a document or ask Tess to do a letter. They were quite relaxed when the two of them went on dates together; it was good for Abe to have a bit of fun with a girl. But when things became 'serious' and Abe talked about wanting to marry Tess, it was a different matter. In their view she was an adventuress, a little working-class girl, on the make. She knew that the Rostovs were wealthy, and she had taken advantage of Abe being lame and shy to seduce him and worm her way into the Rostov family. She is working-class, they muttered to each other, she has no education (unlike our Florrie!) and we know nothing about her family. It's amazing how short a time it takes to turn a family of desperately poor immigrants into members of the bourgeoisie with portable property they need to defend against the cunning of the common people. Tess's parents were immigrants from the old country too. They might even have arrived on the same boat; they had just not been so successful. Jacob and Harry tried to tell Abe he was making a big mistake, but he defended Tess fiercely. Rachel had her doubts too, when she first met Tess, but she could see that Abe loved her and she didn't want to spoil his happiness. In the end, the men gave in, reasoning that, cripple as he was, Tess might be Abe's only chance, and if the Rostovs took her in, they might be able to give her a bit of polish. For my part, I always liked Auntie Tess. She was glamorous with her glossy hair and bright red fingernails; she was lively and pretty and always welcoming when I went round to play with my slightly older cousin, Peter. Florrie accepted her too, although she shared her family's prejudice and would sometimes remind me that she had been 'only the office typist'.

One year later (1935) Benny, back in captivity with the bristles, met the girl he was to fall in love with and to marry. Ada's parents were comfortably off and therefore more acceptable to the family. Her brother was a doctor, a GP but with a higher qualification, the MRCP. Their wedding was a great event, more elaborate than any of its predecessors, with a lavish reception and nearly a hundred guests. Michael and Kenneth, now two little boys aged 10 and 7, were invited as well and Manny had new suits made for them in honour of the occasion. They had their photograph taken at the wedding and Florrie keeps an enlargement of it in a silver gilt frame, on the mantelpiece in her dining room. Michael is fair haired and taller, of course, but slender. He has a protective arm round Kenneth who is sturdier with round, horn-rimmed children's glasses. They look very pleased to be there and it must have been the first time they had taken part in a public family celebration.

Chapter 12
Beside the seaside

From 1931 to 1938 the family had a summer holiday, every year. They always went to Bridlington, a cheerful, unassuming resort on the Yorkshire coast about 50 miles from Leeds. Seaside holidays were popular in the thirties. People Manny knew would come back looking invigorated and sun-tanned and Manny wanted to join in. Florrie was doubtful at first, wondering whether they would find anywhere suitable to stay and whether the children would find the change of scene disturbing. So Manny went off on the train for his first preliminary expedition in June 1931. The sight of the sea exhilarated him, and he strolled happily along the wide promenade watching the families on the beach below him. Further north, the beach came to an end, and the promenade turned into a harbour with fishing boats and pleasure steamers sheltering inside the protective encircling wall. Behind this was the old fishing village and behind that the modern shopping street. The hotels on the front were too expensive but a few streets further back he found a boarding house with a welcoming landlady and he booked in for the night.

He slept well and, after breakfast, he reserved two rooms for the family for the middle of August. Back in Leeds he reported to Florrie and the children. Michael knew all about Bridlington and wanted desperately to go. Florrie had discovered that her parents were also planning to spend a fortnight in Bridlington in August with the newly married Harry and Stella and their two younger sons, so they could all be there together. The Rostovs were all staying in a hotel, but Manny was quite pleased to find that it would be possible to escape from them in the evenings and at breakfast. The first holiday was a great success, and so it was repeated every year until the outbreak of the Second World War replaced the sand castles on the beach with barbed wire defences and concrete gun emplacements.

Each year, Manny made his preliminary reconnaissance visit to find lodgings. Let us pick a particular year to stand for all the Bridlingtons. I shall choose 1935. Michael is now ten and Kenneth seven. They play happily together, although Michael can sometimes tease his younger brother. The journey from Leeds is now by road in Grandpa's car, a Vauxhall. The boys have woken early, full of excitement waiting for the car to arrive. Florrie is also up early, checking the suitcases, several times over, the way she does, to make sure nothing has been forgotten. A loud hooting in the street announces that Grandpa and Grandma have arrived. Harry and Stella will go in their own car. Benny will take his wife Ada, and Abe and Tess. We are the only ones without a car, which rankles with Florrie. Manny used to have a car before the war, but after being fined £10 for speeding he never drove again. Was this an excuse for not being able to afford a car like his brothers-in-law? I am not sure. But getting to Bridlington is no problem as Jacob is very happy to take them. Manny sits in the front passenger seat with Michael on his knee. Rachel and Florrie sit in the back with Kenneth on Florrie's knee. There are, of course, no motorways and the journey seems a long one. The most hazardous part is the ascent of Garrowby Hill which is quite steep for the less efficient engines of 1930s cars. The car goes slower and slower and there are jokes about having to get out and push if it stops. Fortunately it keeps going, although they pass other cars stuck on the roadside with open bonnets and steaming radiators. The ride is a bit uncomfortable with a wriggling boy on her lap, but these are happy days for Florrie. It is lovely to watch her children growing, and Michael is in much better health now with only occasional asthma. If only he were not quite so thin. Kenneth is reassuringly solid and strong despite having to wear glasses.

Once they are over Garrowby Hill, the boys start competing to be first to see the sea. Arriving in Bridlington, they drive through the town until the streets seemed to vanish, leaving only the promenade rail and the sea ahead of them. They drive slowly along the promenade and then back into the town to find their lodgings. By this time Manny has upgraded them to the status of a hotel. Although more modest than the regal Monarch, on the sea front where the Rostovs stay, it is nevertheless a hotel with a proper dining room and a foyer with a hall-porter who carries your bags.

Florrie examines the rooms carefully, hoping not to find anything wrong, like a less than pristine sheet or pillowcase or a leaky tap. She starts to unpack and enjoys the boys' excitement as they persuade their father to take them out down to the beach with their buckets and spades as soon as possible. The sun is shining. It always seemed to shine in Bridlington and they were only rarely troubled by rain. On the beach the extended Rostov-Levinsky family gradually assemble. They have made a tribal encampment for themselves, hiring a bathing tent, a dozen deckchairs and a windbreak. Jacob and Rachel are lying back in their deck chairs enjoying the sun. Jacob is wearing his three-piece suit but has removed his tie and unbuttoned his waistcoat. Harry is there, lying on his side, demolishing an ice cream cone. He greets his lovely Stella who has just come in from a swim, slim and graceful in her black bathing costume, her long dark hair tied up. Abe is beside him, reading the latest copy of *The Gramophone*, his walking stick lying on the sand by his deckchair. Tess is drinking tea from a white china cup and talking to Michael and Kenneth about their sand castle. These two have already built a desert fortress, a complex of buildings with a moat, a defensive rampart and a series of towers topped with fluttering flags. Kenneth is carefully filling the moat with water from a tin bucket under Michael's direction. Manny is setting up the stumps for a game of cricket. Ada, lying on her towel a few yards away, is watching Benny admiringly and thinking how perfect he is. He is crouched behind his latest camera, recording Bridlington 1935.

But there is someone missing. Where's Flo? shouts Benny. She hears them calling her and emerges from the bathing tent in a dark blue costume, holding her rubber bathing cap in one hand and her towel in the other. There is laughter and applause. Benny directs her to her place in the centre of the group. Manny comes to sit beside her and they all settle into their positions with the two little boys in the foreground. Florrie feels a warm glow inside her. She is surrounded by everyone she loves; she feels safe in the embrace of the family. Benny tells the boys to say 'cheese' which they do with exaggerated displays of teeth. He presses the button. If this were a movie, I would freeze the frame and dissolve into a sentimental sepia photograph. Just one more, orders

Benny. Then it's done. Now everyone relaxes. Florrie gets up, hands her towel to Manny for safekeeping and runs lightly down the warm sand for her swim.

Outside the inner Rostov circle, but freely mingling with them, are other Leeds families: the Abrams, the Isaacs and the Macofskis. And even the Millers have come over from Hull for the day. The boys like Mr Macofski who calls them 'Ha'penny' and 'Farthing'. He buys them cornets full of soft ice cream with a red daub of raspberry sauce on the top of the twirl. When these are finished, Uncle Harry takes them up to the promenade to go on the dodgem cars and put money in the slot machines in a vain attempt to win little prizes. Florrie is not too keen on this. First of all Harry is supplying the pennies and they already get 'wages' from Grandpa Jacob. Secondly it's a form of gambling that shouldn't be encouraged. They should be brought up to know how important money is and how miserable life can be if you don't have enough. She is relieved when she sees them coming back. It's getting colder now and Michael is shivering a little. She gets out a thermos flask and pours them each a cup of hot Bovril. Manny, having set up the pitch, suggests a game of cricket to help them get warm again. This is where he comes into his own. He is good at ball games and the other children admire Michael and Kenneth's sporting Dad. Florrie watches him as he runs up to bowl in a very professional way. The Abrams boy (who will become an eye surgeon) connects with the ball and hits it away across the sand. Michael runs after it. The others all cheer.

In those years they didn't spend every day on the beach. Michael always wanted to go on boats and the Bridlington harbour provided many different opportunities. The Uncles would charter a fishing boat, together with its captain, and take Manny and the boys out fishing. This seemed rather dangerous to Florrie, but the fact that Abe went along was reassuring as it was unlikely that they would expose him to physical risks. Sometimes Manny hired a rowing boat in the harbour and took the boys for a trip round the harbour. Florrie would stand anxiously watching them from the high containing wall, her heart lurching as the tiny boat bobbed up and down far below her and seemed about to capsize with every stroke of the oars. She called out to them not to go near the narrow mouth of the harbour, beyond which lay the vast, unforgiving sea with waves that would surely swallow up her entire family. She preferred the trips on Bridlington's premier pleasure boat, an old steam-tug called *The Yorkshireman,* which had been fitted out with seats on its upper decks and a licensed refreshment bar down below. Michael loved *The Yorkshireman* passionately. He would watch it turning to enter the harbour mouth and slowly ploughing towards its mooring. He was entranced by the activities of the crew as they brought the ship up against the harbour wall, tied up the ropes and lowered the gangplank for them to scamper on board. The cruise lasted an hour and took them out of the shelter of the circular wall, into the open sea and along the coast to look at the towering cliffs and the shrieking seabirds. If the sea was calm they wandered happily round the ship or sat eating ice creams. Occasionally the sea was choppy and Kenneth would feel ill and start protesting. How many more hours? he would ask pathetically, as he snuggled up to Florrie. And Michael would whisper in his ear, we're sinking, we're sinking, until his father told him to stop it. Michael was never afraid and never sick. Back at the hotel he would write sea stories in which *The Yorkshireman* had a heroic role, running down pirate ships in the Caribbean and sending out boarding parties, led by Michael, to subdue and capture the evildoers.

Bridlington became a magical place in the family's imagination. Kenneth felt so possessive about it that he couldn't bear to hear anyone outside their immediate circle even mention the name. There were other resorts on the Yorkshire coast. From Bridlington they visited Filey and Scarborough but Michael and Kenneth never wanted to stay there. The Rostovs were loyal to Bridlington too. But what was its appeal to Florrie? She found it difficult to leave home and tended to worry about the house being burgled or catching fire. I do too. Did I learn that unwanted habit of mind from her? But once established in a comfortable hotel, she could relax on the beach surrounded by her family and her friends. The children were happy. Manny could be himself and show off his strengths so that she felt proud of him. And when she felt like it, she could run down to the sea and let the waves wash away her cares.

Chapter 13
The late thirties at home

As the decade moved towards its ominous close, Florrie moved through her own late thirties. Her life was centred on her two boys, now in their middle childhood, pre-adolescent phase between seven and twelve. Michael continued to be thin and delicate looking, laid low at irregular intervals by his unpredictable asthma. In between attacks he was really quite strong and athletic, but Florrie continued to worry about his thin legs and conspicuous ribs. Kenneth with his more compact build was more reassuring to look at and she had to be careful not to admire him too fondly and obviously. She was concerned about Kenneth's rather secretive episodes of naughtiness. She knew that he sometimes stole sweets from the shop where they spent their 'wages'. This consisted of half a crown a week, ceremonially handed over on Saturday mornings by Grandpa. It was more than most children were given so there was no need to steal. Did he do it out of bravado? Was he under the bad influence of other children such as that Barry Stone? Or was Kenneth himself the bad influence?

Her psychological awareness made her wonder if he felt short of love and needed to steal it in symbolic form. One day, when he was about seven, he told her at teatime that he felt there was a cloud over his mind. Remembering Dr Eder's methods, she encouraged him to talk about it.

Tell me more about the cloud. Where does it come from? Is it anything to do with the thoughts in your mind?

There's a thought that I don't like.

Can you tell me about it?

I think I might have been bad. Then he confesses to having taken some copper coins from her purse.

Oh Kenneth! She was taken over by a surge of anger and disappointment with him. What did you do that for? You get all that money from Grandpa.

Kenneth bursts into tears and wants to be consoled. Then she feels she had been a bad, cruel mother, but she couldn't help it. Emotions were so difficult to control. They took you by surprise.

That night, in bed, she tells Manny about it in a low voice so the boys, if they are awake, will not hear. As she tells the story, it occurs to her that Kenneth is probably jealous of his little cousin, Philippa, Harry and Stella's baby. She is now a cute three-year-old with a touch of her mother's beauty. A little Shirley Temple, who could now be seen, sitting on Grandpa Rostov's knee and playing with his gold watch, just as Kenneth used to do.

But most of the time Kenneth was good. After school and at weekends, he and Michael would go out into the yard at the back of the house to play. Their house was part of a terrace in a district that I would think of as poor and working class although, in its day, it was a considerable step up from the Leyland slums. Each house had its own yard reached through the kitchen door and along the back of the yards ran the narrow back street, 'Back Grange Crescent' a sort of humble private thoroughfare which linked the yards and afforded a sense of community. In Back Grange Crescent the boys met their friends, swapped comics and marbles and played football and cricket. Sometimes Manny would join them and be much admired for his style and skill. Sometimes a boy would knock at the kitchen door and say coaxingly: fetch your dad out, which made Florrie feel proud. Yet at other times, she feels a return of the old feelings of oppression and dread. She can't stand the noise and activity of the boys at weekends and just wants to be by herself.

Then she says to Manny, in the old Yiddish language, *Nemen Aben*. Take them away. Take them out somewhere so I can be left in peace. And so he will take them on a tram to the park where they can play ball games, have a fizzy drink or an ice cream, and come back to find their tea ready

Did Florrie have any life 'of her own' apart from cooking and cleaning and looking after the children and visiting her parents on

Saturdays? Yes, she did, but when I try to describe what she did, it seems very limited and unadventurous, considering her talents and her spirited personality. She played the piano, having been given a good grounding in technique by Rachel and her childhood teachers. She made sure that the boys had piano lessons too, and she managed to share her love of music with them by a kind of osmosis. I think that they could feel her enjoyment of it and they opened up to it too. Often, in the evenings, Michael or Kenneth would clamour for her to play (and sing) to them. The piano was a handsome rosewood upright, which said *Made in Dewsbury* above its central keyhole which seemed to imply that it came from Manny, though in fact it had been a wedding present from Rachel and Jacob. It was kept tuned and made a decent sound. What did she play? The recital would begin with 'Buttercup' to which I have already alluded, and perhaps some other Gilbert and Sullivan songs such as 'Take a pair of Sparkling eyes' or 'A wandering minstrel, I'. Then she might go on to some Chopin waltzes. Her favourites (and theirs) were the Minute Waltz and the Waltz in A flat opus 69 No 1. If I play that one on a CD now, its wistful, yearning tune reminds me of her at her happiest and best. I can see her concentrating on the music, then turning to smile at Kenneth who is standing ready to turn the page for her.

But did she get outside the house on any business of her own? She had her friends, those leftover ladies from the carnage of the trenches. They played bridge at each other's houses and they went to the cinema and occasionally to a concert in the Town hall, or a play at the theatre. The Carl Rosa and D'Oyly Carte opera companies continued their annual visits to the provinces. The closest she came to work outside the house was through her involvement in the Women's Homeland Movement, or to give it, at last, its proper name, the Women's International Zionist Organisation (WIZO) This had been founded in 1918 by some energetic young women headed by Rebecca Sieff, the daughter of Michael Marks whose Penny Bazaar in Leeds grew to be Marks and Spencers. Another founder member was Edith Eder, Dr Eder's wife. WIZO's aim was to support the Jewish community in Palestine in its efforts to found a national state. As a women's organisation, it concentrated on social and family issues rather than politics. Those who went to Palestine helped to set up hospitals and clinics, and to look after the welfare of poor families and abused wives. Those like Florrie who stayed at home were engaged in a round of fundraising events. These included 'coffee mornings', lunches with guest speakers, quizzes, dinners and sales. The grandest event was the Blue and White Bazaar held in a large venue such as the Town Hall and aimed at raising large amounts in donations as well as sales. Local WIZO was organised in small groups of contemporaries who stayed together over the years. So Florrie's group contained most of her friends and had an important social and supporting function.

All the same, I am not very impressed with my mother's working life. I can see that she made a contribution to people's lives and I am glad that it was social rather than political. I'm pleased that it gave her something to do and got her out of the house where she could talk to people and work with them. But I don't think it challenged her intellect. She was aware that she was cleverer than most of her friends. She enjoyed reading. She and Manny had a dark oak, glass-fronted bookcase which contained all sorts of treasures, as I later discovered for myself. Manny had bought a complete set of handsomely bound Dickens (special offer from the *News Chronicle*) and she had read several of them. *David Copperfield* was her favourite. She had read Jane Austen and Charlotte Brontë at school. She went to the library every week and was interested in twentieth-century writers such as Galsworthy and H G Wells. She read books about psychoanalysis including books by Freud himself, as well as more popular accounts by analysts such as Barbara Low. She knew what was going on in politics and she and Manny both supported the Labour Party. Only her friend Ray had more radical views which she expressed with great vehemence. When politics came up in family gatherings. Florrie kept quiet and felt embarrassed by the verbal sparring between her Conservative father and her Socialist husband who would provocatively declare that he was a Communist.

So, Florrie, why didn't you do more? You could have gone in to local politics and become a councillor. You could have trained as a teacher or a social worker. Maybe you could have trained as a psychoanalyst; it wasn't strictly necessary to be a doctor – there were several distinguished women analysts who were not medically qualified, including Freud's daughter Anna. I want to ask her what stopped her, but I don't want to upset her. I know that she is easily inclined to disparage herself. I would hate to precipitate another breakdown by being too challenging. But she is reading my thoughts:

It's all right, I don't mind talking about it. You are right in a way, I could have made more of myself. I should have tried harder. But attitudes to women were so different then. If you had children you weren't supposed to go out to work as well. Of course the poor women did, they had to because they needed the money. So you were middle-class by then? Yes, I suppose we were. But some of your friends were professionals who worked. Sarah was a teacher, the White sisters ran a cinema and Rebecca was an orthodontist. I know, but they were all single girls. There were so few young men left after that terrible war, you felt you were lucky to be married and have children. The least you could do was to stay home and look after them. And, you know, I was really quite happy to do that. I wasn't as ambitious as you would like to think. After all what is the most important thing in life?

And here she goes off into one of her favourite little lessons about the importance of loving and being loved and feeling secure and trying to be good to people. I think this was the message that she took from psychoanalysis. Maybe it was bland but it was humanistic and free of dogma and doctrine. It didn't altogether protect her from the darker feelings and the anger that would take her over during the difficult patches of her life. But it remained her underlying belief about how one should live.

Chapter 14
The gathering storm. The new house

My parents and brothers lived through some very significant events in the late 1930s, some of which had more impact on them than others.

The 1936 abdication crisis was of considerable interest and they followed its dramatic development on the wireless and in the papers. Florrie always took the Royal family very seriously, an attitude which I thought absurdly futile in my teens but now I can understand it better. Her parents always felt gratitude to England for allowing them to settle in the country. Jacob was very proud of his citizenship which he had achieved in 1909 with a reference from the local milkman who was willing to vouch that he was an honest man. On the certificate he is described as 'a subject of the Czar'. He was very happy to become a subject of the Emperor Edward VII instead. Florrie absorbed this loyalty to the Saxe-Coburg Windsors as she grew up. On Christmas Day (a low-key celebration in the homes of our people) she and Manny and the boys all listened in respectful silence to the King's speech. She was especially fond of George VI who was brave and somehow vulnerable. She admired the way he had taken over from his errant brother, steadied the ship of state, and conquered his stammer sufficiently to make the annual broadcast. When the King sent good wishes to his subjects 'wherever you may be and whatever your religion' she shed a tear of gratitude and wiped her eyes with her apron before going on with serving the dinner.

Also in 1936 were the Hitler Olympics in Berlin. The boys followed the athletics avidly and cheered the victories of Jessie Owen, the black American sprinter. Florrie and Manny found all news about Hitler and

Germany troubling, like most of our people. But the events were still too far away to rouse serious fears. The Spanish Civil War was also unpleasant to read about but they did not feel personally involved.

And yet, by late 1938, everyone could see that Europe was moving towards another total war. Florrie and Manny read about Chamberlain's negotiations with Hitler and were hopeful. They heard Churchill's warnings and his calls for re-armament but they did not like Churchill; in those days, he had too much ultraconservative baggage and had yet to seize his moment. When German troops moved into Czechoslovakia it was too European an event to bother our established Englishers. But *Kristallnacht* on November 9th was a real shock, with pictures of our people being humiliated in the streets of Berlin by Nazi soldiers. There was much fearful talk of what would happen to our people if Hitler invaded Britain. Florrie's brother Harry made her feel very anxious by talking about taking his wife and daughter to America. (In the end, everyone stayed).

But, despite the deteriorating European situation, something good happened for Florrie and her little family in 1938. They moved to a new house, in the new northern suburb of Alwoodley, leapfrogging socially over the heads of Florrie's brothers and most of the rest of the community who were settled in Moortown, which was nice enough and a lot better than Chapeltown but not on the edge of the country like Alwoodley.

How did they manage it? Partly as a result of Florrie's determination. She had watched her brothers marry and buy pleasant spacious little detached houses in Moortown, where the streets were wider and cleaner and there were no backyards or outside privies. She still felt bruised by their condescending attitude to Manny during their financial difficulties and wanted to go one better. Moortown had been built up in the early 1930s as the city spread rapidly northwards up the Harrogate Road. Now, in 1938, there were advertisements in the *Yorkshire Post* for houses being built beyond Moortown on green field sites.

One Tuesday afternoon (Manny's half-day off) in February he and Florrie took the bus from Chapeltown, four stops past Moortown corner until they were almost in the country. They walked a hundred yards past the shops and then turned right, walked a little further until they came to Sandhill Oval. This was indeed a street in the shape of an oval, built on a gentle slope. The upper half of the oval was built up with detached modern houses on both sides. But the lower half had houses under construction on its outer side only. In the middle of this half of the Oval was a field. The only building was a temporary looking site office with a sign saying: *L Bristow and son, Building Contractors.*

Inside this large hut, Florrie and Manny would meet Mr L Bristow in person, and he would offer to build them their dream house. Mr Bristow was a genial, persuasive man with a weather-beaten face and sandy hair. He showed them lots of plans that they didn't altogether understand. Undeterred, Mr Bristow asked them how many rooms they were thinking of and whether they had any special requirements. Manny looked at Florrie who knew exactly what she wanted. A large square kitchen, big enough for the family to eat in; a similarly large square bathroom; a dining room and a lounge downstairs; four bedrooms including one for the maid. And a garden, will there be a nice big garden? There certainly will, Mr Bristow promised with a chuckle. He made lots of notes. Then he showed them different kinds and colours of brick: orange, grey or dark red. They both like the dark red one best. Then he took them out and showed them some of the houses already going up. There was a vacant plot right at the bottom of the Oval before it started its curving progress back up the hill. The road was unpaved, full of stones and mud and puddles, but they were assured that it would soon be properly surfaced. The most wonderful thing was the view from what would be their back garden. Beyond the back fence was an enormous field in which cows were grazing. After that, they could make out a fringe of tall trees with another field beyond.

As I watch them excitedly anticipating this huge leap forward in their quality of life and social status I look at my young parents and wonder how they are going to pay for this foursquare, proudly detached mansion on the very edge of the city, further into the country than any Rostov had ever penetrated. But I don't want to spoil their pleasure. They walk back to the bus stop, arm in arm, imagining what the new house will be like. They note the little parade of shops and are pleased to see that it has a Co-op where Florrie will be able to buy groceries. She will continue to order meat from the kosher butcher in Chapeltown who she knows will deliver in his van. On the bus they are silent, wrapped in their dreams. Only when they are back in the reality of the house in Grange Crescent, which now looks shamefully poor and cramped with no garden, only a miserable yard, only then do they start making calculations. The house will cost nine hundred and fifty pounds. They will need a deposit of two hundred and fifty and the rest they can pay monthly over 12 to 15 years.

We should get two hundred and fifty from selling Grange Crescent, says Manny. Then there will be the mortgage payments. We'll have to use our savings to top up what we can afford out of our income.

Florrie frowns. She wants to keep the savings which come from 'her' income on 'her' property, the shop in Dewsbury, bought by her father and given to her.

It will be worth it, says Manny, noting that familiar financial frown. What are savings for, after all, but to spend on something really important like this?

Florrie considered. She didn't like the idea of their savings disappearing.. Who know what might happen? Suppose there was another slump? This wasn't a good idea. She made up her mind.

Don't let's use our savings. I'll ask my father to help us. He'll be sure to say yes because he wants to see us better ourselves. Everyone is moving out of Chapeltown now. My brothers are in Moortown and Dad and mother are moving there in a few weeks.

And we shall be farther out than anyone, says Manny with a hint of triumph.

I hope we're not going too far out. I want to stay in touch with Dad and Ma and the family. I wonder how often the buses run.

We could get a car, says Manny. The house will have a garage to keep it in.

But you haven't driven for twenty years! Cars are different now from that old wreck you had before we got married. You might not be able to do it.

I can take lessons.

(But he never did. We all went on using buses or getting rides from Grandpa Jacob. And everyone who called for us in a car, complained about the terrible road surface which would surely damage their springs and was not finally made until 1956.)

As the months passed the foundations were laid and, on the previously vacant plot at the centre of the partially built up hemi-oval, house number 62 began to take shape. It was made of rich wine-coloured brick. Its dark oak front door was guarded by a porch and its front rooms, top and bottom had generous bow windows. On the other side of the door was the garage, which never saw a car, but housed the old wedding-present mangle and other clothes-washing paraphernalia as well as gardening equipment and bicycles. Over the garage was the maid's room. I am embarrassed to think that my parents had maids; it sounds as though they were trying to keep up some sort of pathetic feudal lifestyle. But the girls needed work and lower-middle-middle class housewives like Florrie had one as a matter of course. In the twenties and early thirties the maids were country girls of 16 to 18 from villages around Leeds. In the later thirties they were replaced by refugee girls from Germany.

At the back of the house were the large square kitchen and the bathroom above it. The rarely entered lounge or rear sitting room gave onto a crazy-paving terrace via a pair of French windows, difficult to open. A set of steps at either end of the house led down from here to the large expanse of grass and the flowerbeds. Beyond were the fields. I should also mention that outside and just below the kitchen windows was a solid cubic, brick edifice with a concrete top and a green wooden door in the side. This door led to the underground air-raid shelter which Mr Bristow had prudently provided for all those clients who agreed to pay a small supplement. Most of them did as, by now, another war was beginning to seem inevitable and there were stories about the terrible effects of bombing. The green door was to provide an escape route if the house were to be reduced to rubble leaving its occupants alive in the cellar.

I see that I have described the Sandhill Oval house in great detail. The fact is that I knew the house well and I miss it still. In a few years time, in the middle of the war, I shall be born in the front bedroom and thus enter this story as a character, while still keeping my role as narrator. As you may have surmised, I shall be the third and last of Florrie's children. Yes, another boy. I shall leave further introduction of myself until we reach the proper time as well as the place.

Mr Bristow did not fulfil all his promises to Florrie's satisfaction. Some details were never quite finished in the way she wanted. But on the whole, she was content and looking forward to the move. As tiles began to cover the wooden ribs of the pitched roof and the windows were glazed, the contract was signed. The old house was sold for not quite as much as they had expected, but enough. The mortgage was confirmed by the Leeds Permanent Building Society with a loan of £700 repayable at three pounds sixteen shillings and eight pence a month over a twelve-year term. A second, interest-free lump sum was added to Florrie and Manny's saving account by means of a cheque signed by Jacob Rostov.

They went shopping for carpets and curtains. They bought a complete bedroom set for the boys, with two single beds, dressing table and two wardrobes. The hall landing and stairs were to be fitted with a Persian style carpet in red and blue, decorated with circular medallions surrounded by a symmetrical pattern of repeating motifs. There would be a new three-piece suite for the lounge at the back. The front room was also to have a new suite in brown leather (a present from Uncle Isaac and Auntie Annie) and the old dining table and chairs from Grange Crescent. The kitchen already had the latest kind of range with a coal-fired oven that would also heat water for the kitchen and bathroom. They also bought a new electric cooker.

Moving day was in July 1938. It was very exciting, especially for the boys who were on holiday from school. The remaining furniture, including the marital double bed, was loaded into a furniture van, the family following in a taxi. When they arrived at the gate, Michael and Kenneth tore it open and rushed straight down the side of the house, down the steps, through the back garden and out into the field beyond. Florrie could hear them calling to each other and kicking the ball they had brought with them. She and Manny stood at the top of the steps watching them for a while. Then they went into the house where the removal men were finishing off.

To Florrie's surprise and relief everything seemed to be working. Water came from the taps, the electricity was on and even the telephone was working. She plugged in the new electric kettle, unpacked some crockery and made them all a cup of tea.

That night, she and Manny snuggled together in their familiar old bed in the new front bedroom. It was strangely quiet with no houses opposite and no cars in the street. They both felt a sense of elation that their lives had suddenly been transformed. They had a big house to themselves, with what seemed a huge garden and an uninterrupted view of the country. But in the back of their minds was the thought of approaching war with Germany which the wireless and in the papers said was now imminent.

Chapter 15
Living through the war

I sometime wonder how people managed to go on living their ordinary lives while the Second World War was on. I am thinking of those on the Home Front who were threatened not only with immediate death or injury from enemy bombs but the not so distant prospect of invasion, subjugation and in the case of Our People, transportation to death camps. Keep Calm and Carry On was one of the government's slogans and I suppose that is what they did. Didn't people have nervous breakdowns? Undoubtedly some did, though that is not part of the story we told ourselves about our wartime experience until recently. We now know that may of those who went through the worst of the blitz were badly affected. But for the majority of people, after a while, wartime conditions seem to have become normal. Everyone else around you was coping so you did the same.

How did Florrie and her family manage in wartime? For most of 1939 they were enjoying their new house and getting to know their surroundings. The news was disturbing but did not affect their daily lives. Then, in late August, the political situation began to go downhill fast and couldn't be ignored. There was much talk of German bombs and poison gas attacks, for which gas masks had already been supplied. Parents had been asked to register their children if they wished them to be evacuated, if and when war should break out. Evacuation was voluntary but was in the children's interests, the letter said, implying that it would be irresponsible to keep them at home. In spite of the letter, Manny thought it was unlikely to happen; but Florrie with her sense of foreboding, was not so sure.

The boys returned to school in the last week of August. Michael was already at the City of Leeds (secondary) School but, for Kenneth, it was the beginning of his first term. On the fourth day of school (Thursday) they brought letters home announcing that the whole school would be evacuated to Lincoln on Friday. This was the 1st of September: the very day that German tanks surged into Poland. Florrie was astonished. Her boys were suddenly being taken away. For their own protection, the letter said, but would they really be safer away from their parents? Where was Lincoln anyway? The whole thing seemed unreal. But the news on the BBC Home Service confirmed that it was happening.

Michael and Kenneth were excited and saw it all as an adventure. The letter said they had to report to school as usual in the morning but bring with them a suitcase or a bag of some kind containing one change of clothes and a toothbrush, a comb and any other small articles they might want with them. A bag of sweets was recommended and a favourite toy for the younger ones. They also had to bring their gas masks (which had already been issued earlier in the year) and a label with their name, address and date of birth to be attached to their coats. Manny and Florrie went with them on the bus to school and joined all the other parents and children gathering in the playground. They found a teacher they knew, called Mr Barnes who seemed quite jovial and relaxed about the whole thing.

Don't worry, Mrs Levinsky, he said. I'll be in charge of your two. I'll look after them. We'll get them fixed up with a nice billet in Lincoln. Just for a few weeks until it's all over. By this time there was a line of blue double-decker buses drawn up outside the school gates with their engines ominously running. Children were being organised into lines and climbing on with their gas masks and haversacks. They were supposed to board by classes with their teachers but brothers were allowed to stay together. Florrie was feeling quite bewildered. The unreal feeling about the whole thing was getting worse. She hugged them both in turn and then hugged them together. Take care of your little brother, she whispered to Michael.

Don't worry, Mummy, the elder son replied, confidently. I'll see he doesn't get into any trouble.

I didn't mean that. I meant. If he gets lonely, or scared…

I won't get scared, said Kenneth. If there's gas we'll just put our masks on and I expect they'll have shelters when the bombs start.(They had already had fun testing out the shelter underneath the house, pretending there was an air raid and taking sandwiches down with them.)

Manny shook both their hands, which seemed more manly than hugs and kisses both to him and the boys, and they climbed onto the bus which took them to Leeds City station where they would get on board the train to Lincoln. They were among 18,000 Leeds children to be evacuated that day.

As the bus carrying their boys away disappeared round the corner, Florrie wondered if she would ever see them again. Manny comforted her with a protective arm as they walked back to catch their own bus back to the new house which would now be strangely quiet.

Over their supper that night, Florrie says, All those children. What a terrible thing to do. How will we ever know where they have been taken? Suppose they are in some horrible slum? We shouldn't have let them go. She begins to cry softly. And then to sob. Manny feels alarmed and concerned, as always when Florrie cries, that she might have another breakdown. He tries to find something to say that is both optimistic and grounded in fact.

They'll let us know tomorrow. That Mr Barnes is a good fellow. He has children of his own who are going. And (he suddenly remembers) they'll all be given postcards! So they can let us know the address of the people they're staying with.

Thinking about it, I wonder why they didn't telephone, as we expect our children to do nowadays when they are away. On reflection, I realise that most people did not have telephones at home and a 'trunk call' to a different town was regarded as an expensive procedure, only for occasional use. Still this was a pretty dire situation. Couldn't they have gone to the nearest red telephone box and reversed the charges? If the teachers and foster parents even thought of it they didn't make it happen.

It was two days before the postcard arrived. It was written by Michael with a postscript from Kenneth in his broader, less even script. Michael wrote:

We are staying with Mr and Mrs Bartholomew who are very kind and have a nice house, though not as nice as ours. We are in the same room, like at home and have our own beds. The food is quite good though a little different. School is starting tomorrow. I am looking after Kenneth. Do not worry. Love from Michael. To which Kenneth had added *We are OK. Please can you send my warm pullover. They have a wireless but no piano.*

When she reads the postcard Florrie feels she can breathe again. They seem to be somewhere civilised. They will be all right, they will return. She and Manny might even visit them. She has their address! And they will be safe. They have no fears for their own safety because although there has been a test air raid warning, there have been no reports of any bombs or gas so far. After the postcard, letters began to arrive every week, and Florrie replied to them promptly. Mostly, they were reassuring. They asked for postal orders to buy various small luxuries and a few necessities. They requested favourite possessions to be sent from home. Lessons at the new school premises seemed to be proceeding much as they had done in Leeds. Kenneth illustrated one of his letters with a drawing of German aeroplanes dropping bombs on the maths teacher. Then, after a few weeks, he sent a slightly disturbing letter:

> *Dear Mummy and Daddy*
> *I am afraid things are not going well here. Today I dropped three peas at dinner. Mrs Bartholomew told me to pick them up and I refused. She does not like the way you have brought me up.*

This was followed the next day by a diplomatic letter from Michael, which explained that Mr and Mrs Bartholomew had no children of their own and were not used to boys. Putting the letters together they began to see the funny side of Kenneth's defiance and Michael's reassurance. Subsequent letters suggested that the crisis was over and something like normal life was going on in Lincoln.

There were no bombs there, and at this stage none elsewhere in England. But the whole country was accelerating its provisions for war. Slit trenches were dug in parks and gardens to provide immediate (but inadequate) shelter from bombs. Anderson shelters were distributed to be set up in domestic garden trenches. The cinemas, the theatres and the dance-halls closed (although they were allowed to open again by Christmas). The wireless of course continued, but the Light Programme disappeared, leaving only the more serious Home Service. Florrie had to put up special black curtains inside the existing ones so that not a chink of light from inside a house was visible to assist enemy bombers who might be looking for a town. Food rationing began in January 1940 for items such as cheese, butter, sugar and bacon. As Florrie and Manny didn't eat bacon (except occasionally as part of a Bridlington hotel breakfast) they were allowed an extra cheese ration. Meat, tea, jam, eggs were all rationed (except 'dried eggs' in packets). But you know all about this from reading social history or visiting the Imperial War Museum in London. You may even remember living through those days yourself. If so, you will remember that everyone had a Ration Book from which the coupons were snipped and handed over, together with money, in exchange for food. They were buff-coloured for adults, green for nursing mothers and children under 5, blue for children between 5 and 16. (I had a blue one). Petrol was rationed, but the buses continued to take Manny to his office in Dewsbury. Meanwhile, Florrie's brother, Harry, had enrolled as a special constable and was engaged on making sure the blackout was maintained. Benny joined the army and was selected for officer training. He spent the war commanding an ant-aircraft battery on the South coast and reached the rank of major. Abe, with his lame leg, remained to help his father with the bristle business.

Shortly after Christmas 1939, Florrie had a phone call from Mr Barnes, the schoolteacher in Lincoln, telling her that the Bartholomews were no longer able to offer hospitality to Michael and Kenneth because their bedroom was needed by Mrs Bartholomew's sister and her husband. She was asked to come to Lincoln to help find alternative accommodation. Manny didn't want to miss the occasional customer who still wanted a made-to-measure suit so Florrie went on the train to Lincoln on her own. She was glad of the opportunity to see the boys again. She and Mr Barnes went round the streets of Lincoln in a car with a list of available billets. Florrie was shocked at the poverty she saw, which reminded her of the old Leylands in Leeds. Some of the Lincoln terrace houses still had outside toilets. Some could only offer a single bed for two growing boys. The wallpaper was peeling, the kitchens looked primitive. Some houses had a bad smell which she couldn't identify. But the worst thing was the suspicious hostility of some of the potential 'Aunties' who would clearly much rather *not* have a couple of kids foisted on them. Mr Barnes pointed out that he could insist on their taking the boys if they found a house that Florrie thought would be acceptable. Florrie became increasingly unhappy with the whole idea of evacuation. She knew that parents were beginning to reclaim their children and take them home as the skies remained, for the time being, empty of enemy aircraft.

Mr Barnes, she said, as they returned to the car from another depressing encounter:

You have children. Would you let any of them stay in one of the places we've seen today? Mr Barnes considered the question only briefly.

Frankly, Mrs Levinsky, I would not.

Then I am taking my boys home.

Happy to be back in Leeds, the boys soon recolonised their bedroom and the field behind the house where they met their friends. The City of Leeds School was still closed down but places were quickly found for them at Roundhay School, a state grammar school near the park. Meanwhile the War was getting more serious and impinging more on the lives of people at home. I shall remind you quickly that Chamberlain lost the confidence of parliament and the War cabinet and resigned on 10 May, the day after the Germans invaded the Low Countries. Churchill became Prime Minister. The British army was evacuated from Dunkirk at the end of May and the beginning of June and France fell shortly afterwards. After that people were preoccupied by the threat of invasion; and Churchill's grim but courage-inspiring speeches were heard on the wireless. The Battle of Britain was fought and narrowly won over the skies of Kent in August and on 7 September the Luftwaffe started a campaign of bombing raids on London and other British cities. Leeds might well have been a prime target as it was heavily involved in the manufacture of armaments. The Blackburn aircraft factory was building Skua fighters and A V Roe were making Lancaster bombers near Yeadon aerodrome (now Leeds/Bradford airport).Vickers were making machine guns and tanks and the Royal Ordnance Factory at Barnbow was churning out shells and bullets and bombs. And yet these major targets escaped. There were some bombing raids, which wrecked houses and civic buildings. The first recorded attack on the night of 31August damaged the Victorian town hall. As a child I was told that only one bomb fell on Leeds in the entire course of the war, partly destroying the City Museum. I now know that my hometown's experience was considerably worse. In 1941, there were Luftwaffe raids, mainly in March and April. Houses and shops were destroyed and 77 people were killed. Many more must have been injured. But it seems that there was no sustained campaign to demolish the military factories.

So much for the official history. But how did it affect Florrie and her family? What did my mother do in the war? This was a time when women were being called upon as never before to contribute to the national war effort. They were needed in the munitions and aircraft factories to replace men who had gone into the armed forces. Some joined the Women's Land Army and worked on food production; Others helped to keep the railways and buses running. Some became nurses. To begin with all this work was voluntary and jobs were even hard for women to get. Later, in 1941, there was a kind of conscription with all single or childless women between 19 and 30 having to register for work. Those who were pregnant or had children under 14 were exempt. But you could always volunteer. If you didn't want to work in a factory or a hospital you could join one of the Civil defence organisations or the Women's Voluntary Service (WVS). Women could become Air Raid Protection Wardens (ARP) helping to put out fires and come to the assistance of people who had been wounded or become homeless. But Florrie did none of those things, which I think is a pity because it would have done her good to engage with other people, to use her energy and her talents constructively. Here I go again, nagging her about not getting out and having a career. Oh, I'm sure it was difficult and I'm not accusing her of slacking. She had plenty to do in keeping the home running and looking after Manny and the boys. If I try to ask her about this period she looks thoughtful and says, perhaps you're right. I would have been nervous at first, as I had never really done any thing like that. But I would have got used to it and it would have opened my eyes to the way ordinary people lived. Ordinary people! But weren't you an ordinary person? Of course, she says. And my single friends did volunteer. But those of us who were married with children, it wasn't the thing, it wasn't expected; your duty was to your family.

So they all carried on much as usual. Michael and Kenneth went to their new school from Monday to Friday and played football or cricket in the back field at the weekends. Michael, obsessed with ships, cut pictures from the papers of destroyers and cruisers, corvettes and frigates and stuck them in his scrapbook of the War at Sea. Manny went to Dewsbury to see his customers and also spent time as a Fire Watcher, waiting for incendiary bombs to fall from the sky on to the roof of his building so he and his mates could deal with them. They never spotted any, but I am happy to observe him doing his bit. Florrie cooked and shopped and made beds and washed clothes and folded everything neatly along its creases. She cleaned the house, she scrubbed the kitchen floor, and she polished the silver plated cutlery once a week with the help of the maid. For a time they had a young soldier, billeted on them. His name was Jack Frost and he was one the young men rescued from Dunkirk in 1940 who found himself without a home to go to.

Every few weeks there would be an air raid warning at night. The siren had an eerie swooping up and down sound that still gives people who lived through the war cold shivers when they hear it, even in a radio documentary or a film. It gives me a feeling of dread as well. When the family heard it, everyone would wake up and go down to the hall where Manny opened the door of the cupboard under the stairs, moved the carpet sweeper out of the way and opened up the trap door in the floor. This led by a short flight of stairs to the shelter where they would sit and read or play cards. At first they waited anxiously for the sound of aero engines, droning like large domestic fans, or even the noise of explosions. But when this never happened they just felt rather bored and waited for the 'all clear' siren, a single high–pitched reassuring note with none of that sickening wailing up and down that made the warning siren so horrible. Perhaps the big raids of March and April 1941 produced a distant rumble or a vibration through the earth that could be felt down in our shelter, five miles from the City centre. But they weren't mentioned in the papers because of the need for security.

By March 1941 something else was causing new sensations for Florrie. She was receiving signals from within her body, which she realised were due not to fear but to pregnancy! Thirteen years after my brothers, I will shortly make my first appearance as a character in this story.

Chapter
16 I am born

If you are born after gap of thirteen years in the family sequence you are bound to wonder if you came by accident or design. My parents assured me that I was a wanted child and I was inclined to believe them. If they had not intended to have a child they seemed to be pretty much reconciled to having acquired one and making the best of it. But what really went on in those years in between Kenneth's birth and mine? This is what I think happened. At first they decided that two children would be enough, not wanting a repeat of Florrie's breakdown after the birth of Michael. They made use of the equipment that was available in the 1930s and successfully fended off a further conception. Then Florrie's brothers and their wives began to have children: Harry and Stella produced Philippa in 1936; Abe and Tess had Peter in 1938, and Benny and Ada had Judith in 1939. For some reason, they all decided that one child per couple was sufficient and so the family tree became temporarily narrower. All these babies rekindled Florrie's feminine desire to have one of her own to hold and cherish.

Manny, she says, early one night, as they lie in their marital bed at 62 Sandhill Oval, Manny, I've been thinking.

Yes? What about?

It would be nice if we had another baby. Michael and Kenneth are growing up. And my sisters-in-law have all got little children. It makes me want one too. What do you think? Is it right to have a child now? What if the Germans invade?

That won't happen, says Manny. (How can he be so sure? Things still look fairly bad, with Goering raining bombs down on London and Liverpool, even if Leeds is getting off lightly.) But he is confident. We saw them off when they were trying to knock out the RAF in the summer. Our troops are doing well in North Africa, it was on the News this evening. And the Americans are bound to come in soon. I'm sure we are going to win, just like we did last time.

Florrie smiles, partly to herself. She says, it would be nice to have a little girl (Ouch!)

Boy or girl, either would be nice (Thank you, father).

So they stop using the Dutch cap (which I once found, along with detailed instructions for its use, during one of my secret investigations of her dressing table).

And in March or maybe April 1941, as Leeds suffers its worst aerial attack and the family huddles in the cellar-shelter, Florrie feels inside her the first flutterings of her new baby.

When Florrie's abdomen began to swell, they told the boys that a new baby was inside her. They found this very exciting and were not in the least jealous, perhaps because the full implications of sharing their mother with a late lamb had not yet dawned on them. Kenneth proudly told his friends at school, my mother's going to have a baby! On the predicted day of arrival, Nurse Cox moved into the spare bedroom and supervised the preparations. She had been taken on as a maternity nurse when Tess had her baby and had remained as a sort of family retainer, moving to whichever household had or was about to have a new baby. By the time of my impending birth she had become a trusted friend and confidante of Florrie and her three sisters-in-law.

Two days later, my father was sitting in the dining room reading *The News Chronicle*. He had decided to stay at home that day in case the baby was born. Florrie was upstairs talking to Nurse Cox about nappies and baby clothes. The boys were at school. Then the doorbell rang and Manny went to answer it. He was surprised to see my Uncle Benny in his Army uniform. Home on leave, he had heard about the imminent arrival and had come to pay his sister a visit. As Florrie was busy with Nurse Cox upstairs, Manny showed him into the dining room (our main sitting room for every day, and only used for meals on special occasions, when its handsome, square, polished oak table, guarded by leather seated, high backed, matching chairs would come into use). As they waited for my mother to come down, Manny asked Benny how things were going with the war in general and Benny's anti-aircraft battery on the South coast in particular.

We had an exciting time last week, I can tell you, said Benny. There was a big raid on Wednesday night but we had plenty of warning. We hit three of the buggers and two of them came down in flames. I wish you could have seen it.

Did you actually see the planes crash, asked Manny.

We saw one come down in the sea and the other was trailing smoke and losing height quickly. It looked very sick.

Benny had more to tell of his adventures and they were both engrossed in the subject when suddenly they heard from above their heads the sounds of raised female voices and running footsteps. Hallo, hallo, said Benny. Something's happening up there. Then Nurse Cox came quickly down the stairs, greeted Benny and said to Manny, She's in labour and it's coming on quite quickly. I'll ring for the midwife.

What about the doctor? said Manny.

We'll let him know, but the midwife usually does the delivery.

In the event, the midwife was busy on another case, and it was our old friend Dr Samuel (still in practice after all these years) who came and, assisted by Nurse Cox, brought me gently into the world at about 4 p.m. on October 30th 1941. My mother was 39 and it was the day before her nineteenth wedding anniversary.

Now that I have emerged into the world and become a character in my own story there are some decisions to be made. Can I continue to direct as well as playing a leading part? Now that I am here, should I switch to a first person narrative and tell the story from my own point of view? I am not sure. For one thing I am far too young at this stage to do it convincingly, although I will allow myself a few precocious memories. But more importantly, this is Florrie's story and not mine. Or is it? Some of you will point out that I am telling her story as it is refracted through the prism of my own experience of her, and of our relationship. Well, I said at the beginning that I wanted to get to know her better, and to do this I must see things through her eyes as far as possible. Maybe we will have to share the point of view. This is difficult work. I suggest that, for the moment, and with your permission, we should just continue and see what happens.

ॐ

It was a relatively short and easy labour and Florrie recovered quickly. The baby had fine dark hair and brown eyes and looked like Kenneth rather than Michael. She breast-fed him successfully and they (we) embarked on a joyous mother-infant love affair that would last about 18 months. I smiled at her with my brown eyes and she smiled back with her blue ones. We could get totally absorbed in each other so that the rest of the world did not exist for us. However, we weren't in our trance-like state the whole time. Everyone wanted to hold me and play with me: my father, my big brothers, my child cousins, my uncles and my aunts. In December, the Japanese attacked Pearl Harbour and America came into the war as my father had predicted. The Russians, betrayed by Hitler, were now fighting him from the other side of Europe. Life was still hard and the news headlines grim but the outcome now seemed much more likely to be favourable. I learned to sit up and to test things by putting them in my mouth. I started crawling and babbling, to my mother's delight. Although she had seen all this twice over, she still enjoyed witnessing and being part of the developmental process. She took me for walks in a large black pram, of the sort you never see nowadays, with large wheels and springs, clearly related to the kind of carriage that was drawn by horses. For a while she was happy. And then...

The demons in her depths began to stir again. When I was about a year and a half, she fell ill with something mysterious. She slept badly at night (although I rarely disturbed her) and felt exhausted and drained after very little effort during the day. Her eyes lost their sparkle and she became depressed again. She no longer enjoyed her food. Manny watched her health sliding away with anxiety and a familiar feeling of helplessness. Perhaps having another baby had been too much for her after all. Even the boys could see that she wasn't well, was less responsive and tended to fall asleep in her chair. So the doctor was called in again. Strange though it seems now, my family never went to the doctor's surgery; they always expected him to call on them and, obligingly, he did. Was this a middle class thing? Did patients with lower income and expectations sit in the waiting room or queue round the block? That question must wait for now because the doctor is at the door. This time it is Dr Rummelsburg who has joined up with Dr Samuel. He is puzzled by my mother's condition. She looks very unwell but he can't put his finger on anything. At that time doctors relied more on instinct and less on blood tests. He calls in a specialist who diagnoses nervous exhaustion or neurasthenia. In the confident way that specialists have, he prescribes complete rest for a month (with the help of a sedative), an iron tonic and a special diet. Above all, she must be spared the strain of looking after a young baby. Other arrangements must be made. At first, my father thinks of Nurse Cox, but she has unaccountably disappeared into some other life, perhaps to see her family. The specialist recommends a nursery in the village of Pannal, about seven miles down the road towards Harrogate. They have an excellent reputation and will look after your little one very well until you have made a complete recovery.

And so they took me to Pannal and left me there, in the care of 'Nurses' but separated from my mother, my father, my brothers, my home, everything comforting and familiar. How could they do this to me? I suppose they followed the doctor's well-meaning but wrong-headed advice. I have to concede that John Bowlby had not yet published his influential work on 'Attachment' and the devastating effects on infants of 'Separation.' Parents were still not allowed to visit their children in hospital 'because it upsets the children'. The doctor said Florrie needed complete rest and so that was what she must have. Only by being in close touch with your inner infant could you realise that infants and mothers need each other even if it upsets them.

So my mother didn't visit me for the three weeks I spent in the nursery. Even so it might have been all right if I hadn't developed diarrhoea and become seriously ill. You are going to ask me how much I can actually remember of this traumatising event and my answer is not much. But there are a few persisting images that seem to have lodged in my brain. One is of sitting on a little chamber-pot surrounded by several other children, also on pots, and being told to stay there. Another is of a young nurse who provided some much-needed affection and cried when I was being handed over and put in the taxi that would take me home, more dead than alive. Do I exaggerate? Not much. I don't think that nursery had any idea how to treat infant diarrhoea. Perhaps nobody did in 1943.

When my mother saw me she was horrified. She was overcome by guilt for allowing me to be taken away from her. The memory of what happened stayed with both of us. Whenever the subject of separation came up, or whenever we passed a sign post to 'Pannal' on the way to Harrogate in Grandpa's car, I would feel a shiver of dread go through me and she would say, There's Pannal. I should never have sent you to that place. I can't think how it happened.

And I would say (I am now about 10 or 12 or even 35 and driving her to Harrogate myself), It's all right, I got over it didn't I? It wasn't your fault, you didn't know I was going to get ill.

No, I didn't, she replies, but I should have known that little children need their mother and can't understand what has happened if they are sent away from her.

Did I get over it? I think it left a scar, and it may have led to our angry shouting scenes with each other, later on in my childhood. My own psychotherapist certainly thought that I withdrew into myself after that and kept my emotions under lock and key, not wanting to be hurt again. But I'm not sure that I can accept her hypothesis. Psychotherapists get attached to these notions and perhaps overvalue them. Maybe the trauma of exile in Pannal came back and bit me later. But my recollection is that, once I got over my near-starvation and dehydration, and Florrie had recovered from her brief plunge into illness, we were able to resume our mother-and-baby love affair.

In the mornings I was sometimes allowed to climb into my father's vacant space in their bed and sip some of her morning tea which she poured into the saucer for me. It was unsweetened and although my preference was and is for sweet drinks, I didn't mind. She used to enjoy singing to me as she helped me to get dressed. One of our favourites was a Paul Robeson lullaby, which she transposed from his deep vibrating bass to her light soprano.

Oh my baby,
My curly headed baby
We'll sit beneath the sky and sing
a song to the moo-oon.

And it goes on:

So lulla lulla lulla lulla by bye
Do you want the moon to play with?
Or the stars to run away with?
They'll come if you don't cry.

I was indeed curly headed. There was a photograph of me on the top of the piano to prove it. And I kept my curls until the age of about four, when Manny took me to the men's hairdressing department of one of Leeds's dignified department stores. Here I perched on a high stool while jovial, bald-headed Mr Townsend snipped away until I was surrounded by a sea of curls, just like young Paul in *Sons and Lovers*, when he is sheared by his father. I felt that I had undergone some sort of rite of passage, but Florrie looked dismayed when she saw her shorn lamb returning for his tea. Once the curls had gone, it was easier for her to attack my hair with the fine toothcomb, a painful scalp-raking procedure which I seemed to have to endure more or less daily. I am not sure whether this was because there was a genuine problem with head lice or whether this was just one of her obsessive rituals. However the combing might be accompanied by a song. There was one that began: 'On yonder hill there lives a beauty, who she is I cannot say.' The refrain went: 'Oh, No John, No John, No!' with much shaking of the head which made me laugh.

A grimmer procedure, conducted without musical accompaniment was the removal of splinters from my hands or knees. Florrie called them 'spells' and even though I protested that the spell in question was not hurting me, it had to be removed. I could tolerate its continuing presence but she could not. She pursued it with a sewing needle (previously sterilised in boiling water) digging away at my skin with intense concentration. I moaned and cried, but there was no let up until she had worked the little sliver of wood out and displayed it on the end of her needle.

My toys were limited and rather rough-hewn compared to those lavished on today's children. There was a large, boxy, red painted wooden car (I still prefer red cars), a stuffed elephant called Ernest, made for me by Mrs Kaye, the lady who my father employed to do minor alterations to suits. There was my Mickey Mouse gas mask, fortunately never needed for its original purpose. And some bricks. These all lived in a cardboard box in the cupboard under the stairs, and had to be moved out of the way to open the trapdoor into the cellar when the siren went.

Throughout the later war years, the siren continued to sound its blood-freezing warnings in the night, although much less frequently. The family obediently went down through the trap door to the shelter. But they were all false alarms and after while, if it was in the middle of the night, my parents decided to leave me sleeping peacefully in my cot upstairs while they huddled underground.

Meanwhile, the older boys were growing up and doing well at school. In 1943, Michael passed his higher school certificate in Maths, Chemistry and Physics and was enrolled at Leeds University as a medical student, 25 years after Florrie. Ever since anyone could remember, Michael had wanted to be a doctor. His school friends all knew about it and made jokes about Michael wanting to take out their appendix. Was he consciously trying to fulfil his mother's frustrated ambition? It crossed her mind, but she didn't really think so. It seemed more likely, as she said to Manny, that he had been impressed by all those emergency visits from devoted Dr Samuel to rescue him from asthma attacks. Both his parents were pleased that he would have a profession, and not have to be dependent on the uncertainties of 'business' for his financial security. All the same, I can't help noticing that Florrie's tentative step towards a medical career was to be emphatically ratified by her production of a trio of doctors.

Florrie with parents

Florrie with John as baby

Florrie in old age with great grandchildren

Chapter 17
Post-war years

Eventually, the war came to an end and the country elected its first proper Labour government with a huge majority. Manny was delighted that socialism had come at last. Florrie was pleased too, although I was always under the mistaken impression that she voted Conservative; she always seemed to be tacitly on the side of her father when he and Manny had political arguments.

In the autumn of 1946, Kenneth joined Michael at the Medical School of the University, and so Florrie had two sons on the way to becoming doctors. In that year also, my Auntie Stella, Uncle Harry's wife, became seriously ill. Harry wanted someone in the family to look after Philippa, his twelve-year-old daughter.

Of course she can come, said Florrie when Harry telephoned. She knew that Stella had been feeling weak and ill for several days and had now been admitted to St James's Hospital. Have they found out what's wrong with her?

It's leukaemia, said Harry. I spoke to Dr Jarvis, the blood specialist. He says there's nothing they can do.

Surely there must be something, said Florrie but she knew there wasn't. Everyone had heard of leukaemia, a dreaded disease, rare but devastating, that cruelly picked out children and young people. They can give her cortisone and blood transfusion, said Harry. Improve her for a while. But only for a few weeks, and she heard his voice break on the phone and knew that her strong brother was crying.

Does...does Philippa know?

No. I don't want her upset just now. So please don't tell her that it's anything serious. Just say she has to rest in hospital.

So Harry brought Philippa round with her suitcase. He said, Auntie Florrie will look after you while Mummy is in hospital, so be a good girl.

Philippa was a slim, pretty girl, tall like her parents, with straight dark hair. She was fond of ballet and riding. She seemed to accept what was happening quite calmly. But at supper with the family she asked Michael if he knew about leukaemia. Michael said it was a disease of white blood cells but they hadn't done haematology yet so he didn't know very much about it.

As Florrie served her with soup, she looked up and said, will I be able to see Mummy in hospital?

I don't know, love, we'll have to ask your father.

She visited once and was shocked at how pale her mother looked. She had no lipstick on and her hair was no longer glossy. Did Stella know she was going to die? Doctors told people very little in those days. If she knew, she kept up the pretence and told Philippa that she would soon be better and be coming home. A week later she was dead. When they told Philippa, she was numb and shocked at first, unable to take it in. But when she heard Florrie and Harry talking about when the funeral would be, she dived into Florrie's arms and began to cry. Florrie felt Philippa shaking and trembling with the force of her sobs and wanted to cry herself, but felt that she mustn't. Feelings of loss affected her deeply and made her afraid that she would be overwhelmed by a tidal wave of catastrophic emotion. Philippa clung to her tightly and Florrie hung on, despite wishing that she could be somewhere else away from Philippa's raw grief. It was so unfair to do this to a poor young girl. How could there be a God if he did this to his little ones?

Suddenly Philippa detached herself and ran to her father who was standing helplessly by. Can we go home now?

Not, not just yet, he said gently. I have to make arrangements, get some one in to cook for us. You must stay here a little longer with Auntie Florrie.

And so she did. But on the day of the funeral, she stayed at home with Michael and Kenneth. Children didn't go to their parents funerals 'because they might get upset'.

Stella was only 34. Nowadays it would have been different. She would have had chemotherapy and a stem cell transplant, and there is a good chance that her life would have been saved. Philippa would have been told the full story and been allowed to visit as much as she liked, and if the therapy could not save her, she would have been able to say goodbye to her mother. She would have been allowed to go to the funeral, and she would have been offered grief counselling.

Harry found a housekeeper who proved to be kindly, competent and reliable. He and Philippa started a new sort of life without Stella. In the autumn, Philippa went back to her school in Harrogate. Harry had lots of girl friends to comfort him: he had his Clark Gable looks and he would have been a good catch. But he didn't marry again until ten years later.

Philippa has told me that she was grateful for Florrie's generosity and love. I felt proud of my mother for having conquered her own fear of despair and to have come through for Philippa as a substitute mother when that was what she needed most. Looking back I can see that there remained a special bond between them and a special affectionate way in which Philippa always speaks of 'Auntie Florrie'

Meanwhile I was about to start school myself. But where should I go? Florrie didn't want me to go to the nearest state primary school as my older brothers had done. She discovered that there was little private school run by two genteel ladies, only half a mile away at the top end of the Oval. She had visited the school and liked what she saw. It consisted of a converted house with a garden. There were just four rooms in which the four classes were taught. The boys wore green blazers and the girls had violet-coloured summer dresses. They all looked busy and happy. The teachers smiled on them benignly and bent down patiently to listen to their complicated questions. It looked more like a large home than an institution. After the sending away to Pannal, which was still on her conscience, my mother wanted me somewhere safe, protective and as near home as possible. The fees were modest and Manny agreed to the plan.

Despite having been upgraded, I was not very keen on the idea of school. I would really have preferred to stay at home. So Florrie said we would go and visit the school (which I would like) and meet the teachers but I wouldn't stay. We walked together, round half of our Oval until, at the top we came to a branch road, called Sandhill Crescent. A couple of hundred yards further on we went through a little wicket gate into a small garden with netball posts at either end and approached the school itself. It was a small oblong house, differently shaped from every other house in the area, but not at all threatening. I was introduced to Miss Rider who was tall and thin and slightly stooping, with grey hair that hung down the sides of her face. Her voice was determined but slightly tremulous. She had a little pug dog called Toby who sat in his basket and allowed me to stroke him and say, Now then Toby, which my father had taught me was the way to make friends with dogs. Miss Godfrey was definitely younger, not so tall, with dark hair, grave twinkling eyes and a purple dress with embroidery. She had a soft, gentle voice and seemed to me to be very pretty. As my mother discussed the practical details of my schooling I realised that the game was up and thought that, if I had go to school, this would not be too bad.

And in fact, it was pretty good. But this story is not principally about me and I fear that I have allowed myself to occupy the spotlight and indulge myself in talk about my own experiences. We knew this would be a problem once I came onstage and I am glad that I noticed what was happening before it went too far.

Florrie and her family were now living through the 'Age of Austerity': the period of the post-war Labour government. Manny was very happy to see his political heroes putting their socialist ideals into practice. He rejoiced at the nationalisation of the coalmines, gas and electricity and road transport. He looked forward to the coming of the National Health Service and followed Nye Bevan's struggles with the BMA with great interest. The more Conservative Rostovs were not at all pleased and foresaw national bankruptcy as a result of rigid ideology. No one was very happy with the shortages, but that was the result of the war rather than socialist planning. There was an exceptionally cold winter in 1946-7 which, added to food rationing more severe than during the war, led to the slogan 'Starve with Strachey and Shiver with Shinwell' (the ministers of food and fuel-and-power respectively). I had to plod along a snow-covered Sandhill Oval on my way to school but had fun building a snowman with Michael's help.

Despite the austerity, these were good years for Florrie. Her mental health was stable; she and Manny had a sufficient income, a nice house and three children: two medical students who would have secure careers, and a growing little boy to keep them young. Let me pause to describe her as she was in 1947. She was 45 and in her prime. Her hair was quite long and done in a kind of roll round both sides which was the fashion at the time. She was a little more rounded than she had been in her twenties, but still attractive-looking with her blue eyes and ready smile. Her dress with unpadded shoulders and a longer skirt reflected the New Look style just introduced by Dior from Paris. A modest increase in the clothing allowance now permitted lower hemlines.

What did she do? She shopped and cleaned and cooked meals for the family. She listened with pride and interest to Michael and Kenneth's reports from the Medical School. On Saturdays, we all (except my father) went to Grandpa and Grandma Rostov's for the traditional Saturday lunch. After the meal, the grownups would listen to ITMA on the wireless. The acronym stood for 'It's that man again', 'that man' being the star, the Liverpool comedian Tommy Handley. It was one of the first shows of its kind with fast, wisecracking dialogue, surreal fantasies and beloved regular characters each with their signature catch phrase. There was Colonel Chinstrap ('I don't mind if I do sir') the charlady, Mrs Mopp ('Can I do you now, sir?') and the depressive Mona Lott ('It's being so cheerful as keeps me going') People used to love repeating that one with varying shades of irony. Everyone loved ITMA, even Grandfather Jacob whose cultural background was so different. The comedy was followed by 'Listen to the Band' which my brother Michael couldn't stand, and always insisted on switching off. I quite liked it. I also liked the music of Worker's Playtime, and Housewives' Choice, which my mother had on to accompany her many hours of housework. If I wasn't at school I would watch her, help a little, do some drawing or colouring and listen to the wireless.

Later in the year, Grandma Rachel became ill with a kidney disorder, then known as Bright's disease, which was a generic name for all sorts of inflammatory kidney disorders. She probably had acute glomerulonephritis, which is thought to be a disordered immunological reaction to various factors including the streptococcus, a common cause of throat infections. Nowadays it is rare. In 1947 it was untreatable and Rachel went downhill quickly. Her last days were in spent in hospital and when she died the belongings handed to Florrie included a book of poems by Pushkin, her favourite author. In Russian, naturally. And so I have to take leave of Rachel whom we first met as a spirited young girl, helping her father in a tavern in the town of K, in the empire of the Czar of Russia, and serving a drink to a young man called Jacob. I think that all our family's love of music and literature came down to us through her, and I wish I had known her better.

Florrie's grief for her lost mother was suspended by the need to take care of her father, to whom the news of Rachel's death had somehow to be broken. Harry decided that he should be taken round to his daughter's house where they would sit him down and tell him. I remember that when Jacob and his three sons arrived by car, I was led upstairs by Kenneth in a conspiratorial way. As we waited on the upstairs landing, I was desperate to know the reason for all the secrecy. Then Kenneth put his finger to his lips and I heard a strange sound.

Kenneth said: It's Grandpa crying. They've just told him that Grandma has died. After a while the crying stopped and I was allowed to go downstairs again. Peeping into the dining room I could see the forlorn widower, sitting in an armchair, surrounded by his children, a glass of whisky by his side in case it was needed.

Soon after the funeral, which of course I didn't attend, there was an outbreak of ill-feeling between Florrie and her brothers over Rachel's rather sketchy will. It was all very stupid and petty and concerned ambiguities about who should inherit which of the trinkets that were kept in a display cabinet in her sitting room. There was a Georgian silver tea service, which Florrie knew had been promised to her, and various other items of fine china and linen. And a folding card table with polished walnut veneer and 'Queen Anne' legs, that Florrie also knew should be hers. It wasn't so much the items themselves but the fact that they had been promised and were a way of remembering her mother. Why were the boys so stubborn about it, she wondered. Why did they insist that promises, not in the will, meant nothing? Wasn't it only right that, as the eldest and the only daughter, she should have these things her mother wanted her to have? Why were they so cruel to her? She wept and she wanted her mother to come and tell them, or just to come and comfort her. Manny did his best and his stock with Florrie rose as that of her brothers fell. In the end she was grudgingly given the tea service and the card table. But there was coolness for many months and the brothers stopped coming round to visit. Only when Jacob remarried and they all had a stepmother to be jealous of, did Florrie and her brothers reunite against the common enemy. Years later, when Florrie died, I got the card table in which nobody else seemed to be interested. There was no room in my crowded little house for it and we didn't play cards, so I put it in the car and took it round to my friend Marion who found space for it in her billiard room. When I visit Marion, I check out the card table and tell Florrie that it's in good condition, though rather dusty from lack of use.

1948 was my first year that had a number. It had stamps commemorating the London Olympic Games. I remember some excitement over the Derby. My parents didn't usually show any interest in horseracing, but this year the favourite was called *My Love*. My mother and all her friends were putting small bets on *My Love* and sure enough, to the bookies' dismay, it came in first. It turned out that tens of thousands of women all over the country had backed it.

But Florrie's pleasure in her win on the Derby was short-lived. She seemed to be very angry and irritable in those later years of my early childhood. Perhaps it was the death of her mother. But was that my fault? Maybe I was just being awkward and difficult for reasons of my own. Let us not seek who was to blame but rather try to understand.

I admit that I was a bit irritable too. I seemed to get more particular about what I ate and would refuse food if it wasn't presented the way I liked it. I couldn't stand having gravy over my mashed potatoes. It turned the clean, bland, fluffy potato that I liked into a brown, soggy mud that tasted disgusting. I didn't much like the taste of meat (chicken was a rare treat) and I was picky about vegetables. Of course food was still rationed and a cook's life wasn't easy. My brothers, if they were present, would try to encourage me to eat, in their medical student way by saying: have a bit of protein; now a bit a bit of carbohydrate; now it's time for some vitamin C. Sometimes I would play along. Sometimes I had a tantrum and screamed about the food being horrible. All mothers feel pain if you reject their cooking. It is almost as sacred as their breast milk and contains their love. She would suddenly get very angry and push me out of the back door and lock it, leaving me howling indignantly on the high doorstep. I was always very strong on my human rights, which seemed to me to have been grossly infringed and affronted. Maybe all children have this burning sense of injustice.

Jumping off the step, I would run round to the back of the house and climb up onto the solid block which formed the external entrance to the air raid shelter. This was just outside the kitchen window and afforded a good view of what was going on inside. How long did she keep me out there, while pretending to be untouched by the sight of my angry little face pressed to the kitchen window? It was probably only a few minutes.

On one occasion, Michael came back from the hospital, not knowing what was going on. The door was opened for him and I slipped in quickly behind him, resuming my place at the table. She gave me a look, but that was all. It seems a minor example of seven-year-old naughtiness, but why do I remember it? Perhaps after my early exile at the nursery in Pannal I was hypersensitive to exclusion from home. I remember other battles that were fought between Florrie and me, but I am vague about the precipitating act. I would refuse to do something I should be doing for myself; I would have made a mess which she would have to clear up. I might make an off-hand reply or ignore her. It is enough to trigger her anger and her memory of a whole train of previous misdemeanours. She starts to scold me; she reminds me of past crimes committed and past promises broken; she points out how much she does for me and how little I appreciate it. It's not fair. Her voice rises in pitch and takes on a strident edge which cuts like a rusty blade. Her tirade has a rhythm to it, with frequent repetitions of one or more refrains. I hate this voice so much that I put my hands over my ears and start shouting myself: Oh, shut up, shut up, shut up, can't you shut up. We are both getting hoarse. Then my father, who has been sitting next door, trying to read the paper, my father comes in at last, and she starts on him, as second defendant in the dock. He does nothing to help, he is out all day, he doesn't have any idea of what she has to put up with. I escape from the kitchen and leave them to it.

Poor Florrie, I think now. Why wasn't I nicer to her? Why didn't I think, I must be kinder to my mother who loves me really and tries her best to feed me (if only she wouldn't put gravy over the potatoes before I have chance to stop her). Maybe she was grieving over the loss of her own mother and feeling angry with her for deserting her. And for not being there when all those things her mother had intended for her, those left over bits of Rachel, were taken by her thoughtless brothers who wouldn't give them up. And now all she had was an ungrateful child and a 'useless' husband.

After one of these 'rows' as I called them, she would wear an expression of stony indifference for several hours before gradually softening and becoming again the mother I loved. I never really considered how she felt, during the row. I was just a soldier under fire, trying either to retaliate or escape and feeling quite brave and indignant about the unfair ambush. Would I do any better now, I wonder? I have learned how to listen to patients and to put myself into their shoes, treading softly on their dreams. But it's different with your parents. The gush of anger will erupt and spoil it all. I think I succeeded right at the end. We will speak of that it its proper place.

Chapter 18
A time of transition

In 1946 the University of Leeds had a vigorous academic department of psychiatry in which psychoanalytic ideas and Freudian psychotherapists were welcome. After the war, Henry Dicks, the new Nuffield Professor, assembled a broadly based team of doctors, psychologists, social workers and lay therapists. Among those invited to join was Harry Guntrip, a Congregationalist Minister, who provided what we would now call a pastoral counselling service to his parishioners. Dr Guntrip had a psychology degree from London University and was well versed in psychoanalytic theory, although he had not experienced analytic training himself. Nevertheless, he used Freud's ideas and methods freely in his counselling. He had also written a number of papers on psychoanalytic theory and had a reputation as both a writer and a lay therapist. From 5 July 1948 the National Health Service began, and thus his therapeutic skills were available, on referral, without charge.

So when, alas, Florrie began to sink into depression again in 1949, the Leeds department of psychiatry was ready to receive her. Antidepressant drugs had not yet come in to use and the only medicines available were the old sedatives, the bromides and the barbiturates. Our old friend Dr Samuel had just retired so it was his successor, Dr Rummelsburg, who came to the house at Manny's urgent request. Dr Rummelsburg had come from Germany as a refugee in 1939, learned English, retaken his exams and joined Dr Samuel's practice. He was a taciturn man, perhaps overshadowed by his experiences. He listened solemnly as Manny explained.

She gets like this from time to time; she had psychoanalysis in London 20 years ago.

Did it help?

Oh yes, did her a lot of good. Lately she has been fine, until a few weeks ago when she started, I don't know, getting weepy and not wanting to talk to people. And not sleeping. She doesn't sleep well at all. And she goes over her worries, over and over at night.

So you don't sleep either, says Dr R perceptively. And, she has been like this before?

Manny nods, his face tense. I don't want to leave it too late. She's lying down at the moment. Will you want to go up and see her?

Florrie greets the doctor without a smile. She looks pale and exhausted, he thinks.

He asks her a few questions. He takes her pulse and listens to her chest.

Manny waits in the kitchen. (Where are the rest of us? Kenneth is at the medical school, listening to other chests. Michael who has just qualified as a doctor is doing a House Physician post in Dewsbury. I am at school with Miss Rider and Miss Godfrey. We are all out of the way.)

Dr Rummelsburg comes slowly downstairs and into the kitchen.

I have taken a blood sample, he says, because your wife looks so pale. And I think she should have a chest X-ray to make sure no lung problem is there. But I agree on the whole, with your diagnosis. It is a recurrence of her nervous condition, what we now call depression. Fortunately with the Health Scheme I can refer her to a very good psychotherapist. He is not a medical doctor it is true (Manny frowns slightly) but he works in the University. He is very good man. Very nice man. I am sure she will get on well.

And she did, when she got used to him. Dr Guntrip was a tall, spare, dark-haired man, always smartly dressed in a white shirt, silk tie and well pressed dark suit. Florrie thought wistfully about Dr Eder; how she had loved him and how he had helped her all those years ago. Dr Eder had always been comfortably rumpled. This man with his smart suit was very different. But he greeted her in a kindly way and said she should sit at first and only lie on the couch if she felt like it. She would only be able to come once a week, on the Health Scheme, but he hoped that within those limits he would be able to help her.

How was she feeling? What was going on with Florrie now she was 47 years old and a mother of three? She felt a great tiredness (although the blood test and X-ray had been normal) and a great, almost overwhelming sadness; a yearning for something lost, but she had no clear idea what it was. She had her faithful, affectionate husband. Aware that she gave him a hard time, she felt grateful for his loyalty and glad to have him around; but somehow the passion was no longer there. Her eldest son had survived a terrible sickly childhood, and was now a doctor. This was a source of quiet pride. Her second son was well on the way to the same profession And her 'baby' had been a lovely surprise. Although he could be difficult at times, but that was only natural. So what was missing? Why did she have this aching void in her soul? Dr Guntrip said it was all due to her mother dying and that was reasonable enough. But he also thought that Florrie had unresolved anger towards her mother. He was quite firm about this. Unlike the tentative Dr Eder, he was willing to be several steps ahead of his patient, leading the way. His relationship with his own mother had been a stormy one (she still lived with him in the Manse, his Parish house). He later wrote about how she withdrew from him emotionally when his younger brother died at the age of two. Dr Guntrip's hypothesis about Florrie was that her mother's love had been withdrawn from her when her brother Harry was born. And as soon as she was old enough, she had to be a substitute mother, looking after all three of her brothers, perhaps because Rachel had never really wanted to be a mother. Florrie didn't totally accept this formulation. Even though her dreams seemed to confirm the doctor's view, at least when he interpreted them, she didn't really feel the anger with Rachel that he said was lurking in her unconscious. As she saw him only once a week, the relationship between patient and doctor was not as intense as it had been with Dr Eder. But after all, she told herself, she was a mere girl then and now she was a mature woman. Nevertheless, she was impressed with his keen detective work; he was definitely on her case, determined to get to the bottom of her troubles. And, unlike Dr Eder, he gave her his home number and said she must not be afraid to telephone him if she was feeling desperate. She never did so, but was grateful for his concern and his humanity.

The sessions with Dr Guntrip were on Tuesday afternoons at 3 o'clock. I arrived home from Miss Rider's school at about 3.20 p.m. Since Tuesday was my father's half day it was agreed that he would be at home to welcome me and give me my tea. I was not happy about this arrangement to begin with and made a fuss. Where was Mummy? I demanded. The sandwiches he made were no good at all. He used the wrong sort of jam. I could see that my intransigence and refusal to accept him as a mother substitute were making him anxious.. But then he had an inspiration for a diversionary tactic. He pulled our big wooden screwdriver from the kitchen drawer, stood it on its end and made it sing to me. The screwdriver had a round handle with a flat 'face' so it was not too hard to imagine that it was human. Its favourite song, rendered in the voice of the Scottish entertainer Harry Lauder (yet another Harry), was

> *I love a lassie*
> *A bonny Hielan' lassie*
> *She's as sweet as a lily in the dell*
> *She's as sweet as the heather*
> *The bonny purple heather*
> *Mary, ma Scotch bluebell.*

The song was an instant hit and the Screwdriver played its part every Tuesday from then on. Tuesday became known as 'the day Daddy and I have a terrible time together'. I guess we were both missing our Hielan' lassie. Years later, as I have already mentioned, my own psychoanalyst told me I was jealous of the 'Vronsky- analyst' she was secretly meeting every Tuesday afternoon. Perhaps Manny was jealous too. But as we have seen, there was really no cause.

I see that I have intruded on the narrative yet again with an anecdote about myself. I apologise but really I am unrepentant. Because, ever since we started, we have been seeing Florrie through my half-shut eyes. I am dreaming her story. Without me, there would be no story. Those who might have given you the facts are no longer available, I am afraid; and even their accounts would have been partial and subject to distortion. But don't be dismayed. I think that by doing it in this way we can reveal some sort of truth about Florrie (and me) that would not otherwise have been possible.

After about six months, she brightened up again, and the therapy finished at the end of a year. She and Manny went back to meeting in town for lunch on a Tuesday; and in the school holidays, she took me with her. The venue was generally in one of the city's dignified department stores, which had a restaurant on the top floor. Food was still severely rationed and these were not the best times for fancy meals, but we all enjoyed the occasion, and as Florrie reminded us, it was a treat for her not have to cook. Sometimes Uncle Abe and Auntie Tess joined us, and that made it even more of an occasion. Uncle Abe was smiling and jocular; Auntie Tess made a fuss of me and laughed her silvery laugh. They were on friendly terms with one of the waitresses called Doris, who would whisper to them about having saved a specially choice cut of meat for us. Maybe even some chicken breast. After the main course, the ladies usually had tinned fruit salad or jelly while Uncle Abe and I ordered treacle or chocolate pudding.

By 1950, all three of us children were approaching turning points in our lives. Michael had been qualified for two years, had done his pre-registration year and was planning a career in obstetrics. However, he had an unhappy experience as a junior obstetrician in Huddersfield. The consultant staff were at odds with each other and the midwives and there was a shortage of middle grade (registrar) doctors to support Michael, who was the most junior and had very little experience. After being left on call alone for several nights, trying to cope with dangerous situations where the lives of both mother and baby were at risk, he decided he had had enough. He opted for general practice (his original choice) and was doing a traineeship with a GP practice in Leeds. Kenneth was due to take his final exams in the following year. He now had a girl friend, a fellow student called Nettie. They were joyfully in love and wanted to marry. Manny and Florrie thought that they were too young, but they did get married the following year, soon after Kenneth had qualified as a doctor.

And me? I was eight years old and about to leave the cosy world of Miss Rider's for the Leeds Grammar School, an environment in many ways uncertain and unsafe, though promising a good education at a place of high repute. Why did Florrie and Manny send me to a fee-paying school, when the older boys had both gone to a state grammar school? I had read many stories in which the youngest of three sons inherits the kingdom and I'm afraid I took my privileged treatment for granted. The real reason? They undoubtedly had more money by then, but they were still hoping I would win a scholarship when I moved up after two years, from the Junior to the Senior School, so there would be no more fees. Or was Florrie still trying to shelter me from the rigours of state education? I certainly found the Grammar School rigorous enough. Some of the things that went on there – well, they wouldn't be allowed nowadays. For the moment I shall say no more.

Chapter 19
Three go exploring together

When family holidays resumed in 1946, the obvious thing was to go back to Bridlington. By this time my big brothers were no longer interested in sitting on an English beach; their idea of a holiday was something that involved climbing in the Lake District or hitchhiking to France and Italy. Holidays were about going off with a group of friends, including whenever possible, girl friends. So, for holidays, we became a nuclear family of three. I had my parents to myself. For the first few years we continued to go to the seaside resorts of the Yorkshire coast. Please don't think that we went to Bridlington every year. My parents were a little more adventurous. We tried Bridlington's neighbours, Filey and Scarborough. One year we went to Southport on the West coast where Manny's brother, Bertie, his wife Ray and their children, Beryl and Roger, were now living. We even tried Blackpool. However, none of these places, in my opinion, could compare with Bridlington. Our last visit there was in August 1950. After that I had to recapture the experience by taking my own children there, and of course, they loved it too. I think it was mainly the boats. Nowhere else had such an exciting harbour with charismatic vessels like the steam-driven *Yorkshireman* (dirty British coaster) and its more refined, diesel-powered sister, the *Yorkshire Belle*. There were also the *Britannia* and the *Boys Own*. Rumour had it, there had once been a *Girls Own*, but it had sunk. How, when and in what circumstances this happened, if true, I never found out.

Then, in 1951, Manny decided that it was time to go further afield. It was the year of the Festival of Britain, the Labour government's attempt to get us into a feel-good mood and make us forget the long years of post-war austerity. Just to summarise, austerity involved a chronic shortage of interesting food (without malnutrition); clothing and sweets still on the ration; fuel and power shortages; a terrible winter in 1947; economic crises; everything going for export to pay for the American loan; the perceived inefficiency of our newly nationalised industries; the spivs taking advantage (although it was worth knowing one or two of them) and the general drabness of everything compared with memories of pre-war days.

The Festival would celebrate our pride in being British, for having come through the war, our still being a great manufacturing power and having a unique, whimsical sense of humour. And a sense of community, let's not forget that. It began with our all pulling together regardless of class, during the war, but it was cemented by the Labour government which came in on huge wave of enthusiasm in 1945. By 1951, Attlee's government might be on its last legs, but he, Bevin and Cripps had taught us something about the mutual warmth and respect that went with democratic Socialism. And of course there was the National Health Service. I rest my case.

Manny was excited by the idea of the Festival and wanted to see it for himself. Although there were to be local celebrations, the real action would be in London, at the South Bank Exhibition. He had seen pictures of the Dome of Discovery and the Skylon and the illuminated Tree Walk in the Battersea Pleasure Gardens. He wanted to go. Florrie was more doubtful. London was a long way away and very expensive. She had heard that the exhibition wasn't all that good, anyway despite the vast amount of money spent on it. And what about John? He would find it boring and would much rather be at the seaside. Manny's solution was a week in London followed by a week in Bournemouth. This was a shrewd card to play, as Jacob and his second wife had now started to take their holidays in Bournemouth (they favoured the Green Park Hotel, which boasted a kosher kitchen as well as four star comfort). Florrie agreed. Manny went ahead and started writing letters to hotels, and phoning the station about train times.

When the day of departure came, Florrie was rather tired after a disturbed night worrying about whether she had packed the right clothes for us all. A taxi came and took us the Central Station. It was smaller than the City station, but had higher status as it was used exclusively by London trains. Manny had told Florrie that he had booked seats on the

Yorkshire Pullman. She had never been on this train before, although she knew that her Dad used them for his business trips to London. We were greeted by a uniformed steward who looked at Manny's tickets and directed us to a coach called 'Pauline'. The seats were like two double armchairs facing each other across a table with a pink linen cloth and pink shaded lamps. It was more like a sitting room than a train. I was allowed to sit by the window and was clearly relishing every moment of the experience as the engine started huffing and puffing and the train slowly gathered speed. Florrie relaxed in her seat at last and smiled across at Manny.

Aren't you clever, she said to get us on a train like this. Was it very expensive? Don't tell me, I don't want to know.

This was a new Florrie, recklessly abandoning herself to the thrill of extravagance. We both loved to see her in that mood, with the smile creases at the corners of her eyes and her mouth opening in a big smile to show her nice teeth. When lunch was served she could see that I was fascinated by the waiter who was ladling soup into a big china plate in front of me and offering me a bread roll out of a basket, as the train rattled along and the landscape rushed by. She remembered her trips to London to stay with Harry and Dolly and to see Dr Eder. Those journeys were in crowded third class compartments with a corridor down the side. The Pullman was so much nicer. The meal was over now and I was busy writing down the names of each station we stopped at: Doncaster, Newark, Grantham, Peterborough... She read her novel (*South Riding* by Winifred Holtby), she gazed out of the windows, she listened to my urgent requests to get out and look at the engine, when we stopped at Doncaster. She told me I would have to wait until we got to London, as they didn't want me jumping out and having the train go without me. Manny was looking through his guidebook, and occasionally checking his pockets to make sure he had all the tickets and hotel reservations.

When we arrived at King's Cross it was much like the Leeds Central station, only bigger and noisier. A porter took the luggage and we walked up the platform towards the barrier. I raced ahead to look at the steam engine. When they caught up with me, I he started excitedly pointing at it and trying to tell them that it was a very special engine. Instead of the irregular outline of rounded dome and sticking up funnel, it had a beautiful, smooth, streamlined curve from front to back, with just a short square outlet for the smoke. Its nameplate said 'Sir Nigel Gresley' and I proudly informed them that ours was the very engine that had broken the world speed record for a train in 1937. On the other side of the barrier people were milling about, rushing past and nearly colliding with each other. The porter appeared with the luggage and was paid. We gathered round the cases and Florrie saw a large policeman smiling at us. She asked him what he thought was the best thing to see in London. He replied without hesitation: Six pints of Worthington, Madam, all in a row. This restored Florrie's good mood, which was beginning to fray a little in the confusion and acrid dust of the station.

I think I shall stay with my own nine-year-old's point of view now, as it will be easier. When my mother and I are in a scene together it gets difficult to stay inside her head. Especially as I remember parts of this holiday vividly. It was my introduction to London and probably the reason why I ended up living there. Everything about London was special. The taxi which carried us to our hotel was a proper London cab (Leeds taxis were ordinary saloon cars with 'taxi' on the roof.) The streets had names out of Monopoly. The policemen had a sense of humour and you could talk to them. I had never spoken to a policeman before. You couldn't speak to the magnificent guardsmen who stomped up and down outside Buckingham Palace but you could stand and gaze at them and they didn't mind. I took photographs of everything with my clunky box camera (present from Uncle Benny). I have pictures of a taxi, a policeman, and a London bus as well as snaps of Buckingham Palace and Tower Bridge. In Trafalgar Square, I was delighted by the pigeons who were happy to sit on my arm as they pecked corn from my hand with their tickly beaks. The photograph shows me wearing my new Grammar School uniform with cap, blazer, short trousers, long socks and sandals. I was having a fantastic time and I think my parents were enjoying it too. Were they just getting pleasure out of showing London to me and seeing it shining in my eyes? Sure they were, but they also enjoyed being with each other, doing something a bit more adventurous, and not being anxious. Florrie, as we know, suffered from anxiety that was easily set off by hints of insecurity. Manny had to be on watch for the first signs of her trouble so that he could try to head it off. I had some worries about school – but it was the holidays and school was far away, even though I was still wearing my school cap and blazer.

Eventually we took the Circle Line tube (my favourite) from Sloane Square to Westminster, crossed the bridge and visited the South Bank Exhibition. We admired the elegance of the Dome of Discovery, but found the contents a little disappointing. We gazed up at the *Skylon*, a huge vertical object, like a very slim cigar, pointed at both ends and supported only by thin wires. Manny and I consulted the catalogue and decided where to go next. *The Lion and the Unicorn* sounded exciting; but there were no mythical beasts fighting each other like in *Alice*. We had a nice lunch in an enormous cafeteria with the novelty (for me) of self-service. I kept pestering them to take me to the Battersea Pleasure Gardens, and eventually, at about teatime, we did go. It was a park with avenues of trees rather magically lit with strings of electric bulbs. Inside was a funfair and the cartoon-derived Emmet railway, symbolic of English eccentricity and whimsical humour, And you could ride on it which was the important thing.

After all this, Bournemouth was a disappointment – for me. It was altogether too tame and refined, without Bridlington's garish primary colours and slight edginess. And there were no proper boats.

In the following year, 1952, we went to Paris! This was all part of my father's plan to introduce us to the wider world. He proposed the idea to Florrie, who was predictably dubious. She had a pre-war picture of Paris as somewhere colourful, exciting and a bit naughty. This was partly overshadowed by wartime Paris, with German troops marching down the Champs Elysées and having to be liberated by our soldiers. Free now, but probably still dangerous with Nazis lurking about.

So Manny set off on a reconnaissance mission to check that Paris was safe. In June, he took a few days off, crossed the Channel, caught the train from Dieppe to the *Gare du Nord* and found the hotel he had chosen from the guidebook. He had a two-night stay there and enjoyed himself finding his way round and looking at the famous sights of the city. It was quite a brave thing to do as he had never been out of the country before and spoke only a few words of French. By the time he was back on the train to Dieppe he felt that he had a working knowledge of tourists' Paris; and he looked forward exultantly to showing us his discoveries a few weeks later. My Dad was not just a tailor from Dewsbury, he had become an habitué of the boulevards of Paris. Just like Maurice Chevalier in *Love Me Tonight*. Now he would return to Paris bringing Princess Florrie with him (and me of course).

Well, all right then, she said. And in late July we all set off together. We went to London on the Pullman again. We got the boat train from Victoria Station to Newhaven. We went on board the *Arromanche*, a sturdy little vessel not much bigger than the *Yorkshireman*, and sat on deck in balmy weather as the boat ploughed across the channel to Dieppe. I took lots of pictures, little rectangular black and white ones about three inches by two. I still have them in a small blue album. We reached Paris in the evening and had a taxi ride along the right bank of the Seine with Manny pointing out Notre Dame and a distant view of the Eiffel Tower. Our hotel was in the *rue Croix des Petits Champs,* near the *Palais Royale*. It was called, inexplicably, *Hotel de l'Univers et du Portugal* and to Florrie it looked small and shabby. To Manny it was a part of the Paris he now knew and loved. Our rooms were just about acceptable but she didn't like the dining room. The waiter looked scruffy, the décor was dingy, the tablecloth not quite clean and covered with the crumbs left by a previous party. Then the scruffy waiter, with Gallic nonchalance, brushed the crumbs into Florrie's lap. Amazingly, this appealed to her sense of the ridiculous and she began to laugh. The waiter laughed too, and apologised. Florrie gave him a smile. Manny and I looked at each other with relief. We knew that the holiday would now be a success.

We walked all over the city. We rode on real Paris buses with a platform at the back like you don't see any more. We rode on the Metro which had an entirely different smell from the Tube. We ate croissants. We drank real coffee. We went up the Eiffel Tower (more photographs). We went round the *Louvre* and Florrie told us all about the Mona Lisa and the Venus de Milo. We got the Metro up to *Place Pigalle* and Florrie told me all about Henri de Toulouse-Lautrec and how he liked painting the dancing girls. Up the steps we went to Montmartre where there were living artists, painting views of the little square. We bought reproductions. Florrie resolved to do some oil painting herself when we got home. She was loving it. She was in such a good mood the whole time, after the crumb-brushing turning point. We went on a bus tour to Versailles and heard all about the Sun King in his Hall of Mirrors. Saw his statue on a horse (photograph). The best picture I took was of my Mum and Dad posed on either side of a huge vase in the gardens, their hands joined across the front. Even Uncle Benny praised it. It was enlarged to postcard size, framed and given its own place on the mantelpiece next to the two boys at the wedding. On the next day I lost my camera in the Metro and never saw it again. Florrie and Manny were both very keen to get it back and we had to retrace our steps through all the stations, asking the Metro staff had any one handed in a camera? I found my parents' diligence in this matter both tedious and embarrassing. I had already written the camera off and was thinking about its replacement. Besides, their French was obviously not good enough and the kindly Metro men found it quite puzzling. The end came when one of these admirably patient men asked, in English 'Is it a grown man you have lost or a small child?' We learned that the French for camera was not 'camera' pronounced with a French accent, but *appareil de photographie*. We all had a good laugh and I opened the discussion with my Dad about my next *appareil*.

On the last day, Florrie and Manny broke it to me that they had tickets for the *Folies Bergères* which they said was a kind of theatre. I would have to stay in the hotel because it would finish very late and was not suitable for children. (How old was I? nearly 10.) Somehow I knew without them telling me that it was tall girls with long legs, and bare breasts and ostrich feathers that both hid and revealed. Now you see them, now you don't. Why would they want to go and see such a show? They explained that it was typically Parisian and the kind of thing you would never see in England. The costumes and the music and the dancing would be top class.

So why can't I go?

I've told you it's not for children. Anyway, you wouldn't be allowed in.

I had a horrible night on my own. I had a big double bed to myself in the room next to theirs. I woke in the night and wanted a drink, but I couldn't find my way out of the bed. I seemed to have turned through 90 degrees and what should have been the side of the bed was an endless stretch of mattress. I was so glad when they came back and rescued me.

The year after that (1953) we went to north Wales and stayed in Llandudno. Again we had a good time but I remember one strange episode on the train coming home. We were in a corridor train and had a compartment to ourselves. I was now 11. Somehow Florrie and Manny started quarrelling. I can't remember what it was about but it had the familiar pattern of her repeated complaints about something done or not done and what she had to put up with and it wasn't fair. She did this and she did that and she got no recognition, he wasn't doing what he should be doing. Manny's resistance, passive at first became more disgruntled and soon he was raising his voice too, which was quite unusual. I sat opposite them, appalled at what I was seeing and hearing.

I felt that I ought to intervene. I said, why are you shouting? Don't you love each other any more?

The effect was more dramatic than I expected. The shouting stopped instantly and they both looked at me. My mother began to cry. My father comforted her with an arm round her shoulders and my mother tried to explain to me that they did still love each other but that sometimes people who loved each other became very frustrated (one of her favourite words) and angry and behaved badly and they hadn't meant to upset me and I mustn't worry about it and so on.

In the following year (1954) we all had our first flight, on a Vickers Viscount turboprop airliner. We went to Lugano in southern Switzerland and had a happy time in what must have been a very expensive hotel by the lake. That was the last time we all went on holiday together. In the year after that, when I was 13, I went on a school trip to Italy and fell in love with Venice.

Chapter 20
Two young doctors

During the 1950s Florrie was mainly preoccupied with the efforts of her two elder sons to get themselves established as doctors. I was turning in good exam results at the Grammar School and tended to keep any troubles I had to myself.

Meanwhile, my big brothers were also falling in love. Although Kenneth was the younger, he was the first to get married.. He and Nettie met at Leeds University where she was studying French and Economics. They were engaged in 1951 and planned to get married later the same year.

I liked Nettie who was full of jokes and ideas and fun to talk to. My only problem with Kenneth was that he wanted to spend time with his fiancée when he could have been entertaining me. When I complained that they were neglecting me, they both promised that, when Kenneth's exams were over, they would spend a whole day with me, doing whatever I wanted. When the day came, I decreed that we should spend it playing 'Monopoly'. If they found this tedious, they didn't show it.

Nettie's mother (who was a professional caterer) arranged a full scale wedding party for them with dinner and dancing. I was very proud to be invited (I had a personal, hand-written invitation from Nettie). It was, at the age of nine, the first wedding I had been to, and I was impressed by all the white tablecloths, the ample food, the speeches, the band, the dancing. After their honeymoon, Kenneth had to start his first house job at the hospital in Wakefield. National Service in the armed forces was still in operation, but his had been deferred until after his first year as a qualified doctor. Nettie and he shared married quarters at the hospital. I shall leave them there while we look at the beginning of Michael's career.

Michael was exempt from National Service because of his asthma. He had qualified in 1948, and after his house officer year, he wanted to specialise in obstetrics and gynaecology. But after his unhappy experience in Huddersfield (described in the last chapter) he decided to go into general practice instead. This was the kind of medicine that attracted many students who had good memories of kindly doctors who attended them as children. But the hospital consultants told them that GPs were a lesser breed of doctor, whose knowledge was limited and who spent their time with trivial illnesses unworthy of a consultant's attention. Anything really interesting, they were told, was referred to the hospital doctors at once. The GP's letters, scribbled in haste at the bedside, in poor light, at 3 a.m. with more calls waiting to be done, were held up and read out in tones of contempt to the little group of students clustered round the great man.

The training to be a physician or a surgeon was long and the outcome uncertain; there were relatively few consultants in the new Health Service and vacancies were scarce. Many young graduates gave up after a few years and went into general practice (which in those days came with little or no further training) as a reluctant second choice. But Michael was not downhearted. He accepted that obstetrics was not going to be for him and returned quite happily to his earlier vision of himself as a family doctor. To begin with he took a job as a trainee assistant with one of the Leeds GPs. At the end of a year's apprenticeship he continued as a salaried assistant 'with a view to partnership'. However the promise of partnership kept being postponed, as often happened. The NHS strictly limited the number of principal GPs in each area in accordance with the size of the population they were to serve. Each principal was allowed to have up to 3000 patients, far too many by today's standards when the ratio in cities is more like 1500 per doctor. If the area was 'closed' to new principals it was impossible to start your own practice, and existing principals could only take a new partner to fill a retirement vacancy. And in any case, his boss was rather hoping that his nephew, still a student, would fill any vacancy that arose. So although Michael enjoyed the work he was anxious about the prospect of many years on the low wage of an assistant.

He was also married by this time, to a bright and lively sociology student called Pat. Florrie and Manny found Pat acceptable, especially as Michael was older and Pat had a quieter temperament. But everyone said he needed to find a practice of his own. He and Pat turned to the jobs pages of the *British Medical Journal* every week, hoping to find a vacancy in Leeds, but there were none. Eventually they decided they would have to accept something further away. One week, there was an advertisement for a new practice in Hull, some 60 miles away, then a thriving port city. It had been heavily bombed during the war, many working class houses had been destroyed, and the dockers and trawlermen and their families were being re-housed on new estates to the east of the city. Three doctors were required (the advertisement said) to serve this area. They would each be given a new council house in which to start their individual practices. This was an exciting prospect for Michael, as he would be working for himself as a principal and would have the chance to organise a practice just the way he wanted it. He and Pat studied the advertisement over breakfast.

What do you think, said Michael. How would you feel about living in Hull?

Well, I would rather stay in Leeds and so would you. But we look in the BMJ every week and there's nothing! If we went to Hull you could have your own practice, to organise just the way you want it.

But what about our parents? And our friends? We don't know anyone in Hull.

We know a few people. There's your cousin Ethel and her husband. I'm sure we'd make some friends. And if we didn't like it we could come back.

That's true.

Oh come on Michael, it's worth applying for anyway.

(Secretly, she thought that it would do Michael good to be 'rescued' from his parents whom she saw as cold and lacking in affection.)

So Michael sent off an application and was duly called for an interview. He had by now acquired his first car, a rather ancient Ford with a maximum speed of 29 mph. Its registration number was EDU 271. I remember that number because I was very proud to see that we had a car parked in our drive which actually belonged to our family and not to Grandpa or one of the uncles. For years I had felt ashamed of the low social status assigned to me by my school friends when they discovered we had no car. At last this humiliation was wiped out, if only by a ten-year old banger. But could the old Ford be trusted to get him to Hull in time for the interview? While he was thinking about this, Grandpa Rostov offered to drive him there personally. This was a kind, grandfatherly action, but he was also elbowing Manny aside and saying, I'd better make sure my grandson gets to his interview there as you don't have a car and I do.

The interview was a brief one and Michael was appointed to one of the three new practices. He and Pat were delighted. It was a great adventure, and they thought that they would move back to Leeds after a few years but they never did. Michael now had a new car (he would need something reliable for his new practice). I remember that one too. It was a dark-green Austin, a rather sleek, streamlined looking new model called the A40. Michael and Pat set off in it one winter morning with their luggage piled in the back to start their new life. They found the Bilton Grange estate in East Hull and their new home, one of hundreds of neat little brick houses which seemed to stretch for miles and were still being built. Their house had mud up to the front door, according to Pat. Once inside, they found two rooms and kitchen downstairs with two bedrooms and a bathroom upstairs. All the rooms seemed tiny. Somehow the ground floor had to provide a consulting room, a waiting room, space for records and storage and living accommodation for Michael and Pat. At this stage they could not afford to live anywhere else. GPs received a very small 'basic allowance' of three hundred pounds a year and the rest of their income depended on the number of patients who registered with them. Roughly speaking, you needed a thousand patients on your list to earn £1000 a year. Michael's list would start at zero and there would be no 'capitation fees' (fees per patient) for three months.

They decided that the front room would be the consulting room by day and their sitting room by night. The hall would be the waiting room and the dining room at the back they would keep to themselves. And so they moved in and waited for their patients. Each day a few people would knock at the door and bring their NHS card to register. Some were elderly retired workers and their wives, others young families with children. Michael welcomed them all. At first he hadn't much work to do, but after a while the registrations began to accelerate and he was busier. Every week he would drive to the office of the Executive

Council and hand in his latest bundle of cards. The numbers on his list reached three figures and then several hundreds. By the end of the first quarter (when he received his first pay cheque) it was over a thousand. Each week Michael wrote home to Florrie and Manny. (We still didn't make long distance phone calls very often.) He finished each letter with the latest total number of registered patients. We all enjoyed watching the numbers creep up, showing that Michael was a popular doctor and that he and Pat were making a living. Florrie's recurrent anxiety about financial ruin was appeased. But she missed having both her elder sons away. Not only were they married, but they were living in different parts of the country. She hoped that Michael and Pat's stay in Hull would be a short one and that they would soon come back to Leeds and be offered the practice that Michael deserved. He had struggled so hard as a child with his eczema and then the asthma. And he was always so thin. He hadn't found studying quite as easy as Kenneth and he had worked really hard at his books. And now he was qualified, it seemed so unfair that there was no practice for him in his own town; that he had to go into exile while others seemed to have no problem, probably because their fathers were doctors.

To me, there is something inspiring and invigorating about seeing a young couple starting out in life and leaving home to seek their fortune and make a go of things. There are risks and hardships, but they are in love, they are doing it together and everyone feels like cheering when they succeed. We began with Jacob and Rachel making that big decision to leave the empire of the Czar and cross the sea to England; Florrie and Manny struggled with economic and psychological depression in the 1920s; and now Michael and Pat were no less bravely setting up a practice in a small town that seemed a long way from home.

The work of an urban GP was hard in those days. Michael had a morning surgery, followed by up to ten home visits and another surgery in the evening. Then he was on call every night, seven days a week. After a while he and one of the other doctors arranged a rota and he was able to have some time off. I used to enjoy going to stay with them as an 11 or 12-year-old. Michael would take me out on his visits and let me come in and meet some of the patients. Perhaps that encouraged me to become a GP as well.

Meanwhile what was happening to Kenneth? A week after Michael and Pat's wedding he had started his two years of National Service. As a qualified doctor, he went in as a Lieutenant and eventually became a Captain, to my great satisfaction.

Nettie was pregnant by this time and she gave birth to a boy (Jeremy) while Kenneth was on leave. Florrie was very excited and pleased to have a grandson, and relations between her and Nettie improved for a while. After his basic training, Kenneth was posted to the Women's Royal Army Corps (WRAC) depot in Guildford. Here, his job was to be the doctor to a camp full of young women. The duties were light and consisted mainly of a daily Sick Parade which lasted usually less than an hour. Most of the girls were very fit, although occasionally one fainted, though whether out of love for my brother, we weren't sure. At any rate, Nettie, with her new baby, wanted to be with him as soon as possible to forestall any temptation, and they found a nice ground floor flat with a garden and a cedar tree. Once he had got used to being saluted by serried ranks of young women in uniform, life as an army doctor was not very exciting. Sick Parade was over by 11 am and there was not much else to do. But he and Nettie had each other and their baby. They enjoyed their garden and their regular trips to London.

By 1954, Kenneth's army service finished and he too began to look for a practice. During his visits to London in the army years, he had made contact with Florrie's cousin Henry Rostov, who had a GP practice in Willesden. You may remember that we first met Henry as a lad of 20, telling Florrie about the delights of being a medical student. Now Henry needed some help in his practice and he offered Kenneth the job of 'assistant with view to partnership'. Kenneth and Nettie both liked the idea of living in London and they were given the flat above the surgery to start with. All went well at first; Henry was brisk and Rostovian but a capable doctor from whom Kenneth was able to learn a lot. However, the surgery facilities were a bit primitive when he first arrived. There was no hot water in either of the consulting rooms until Kenneth insisted that 'Ascot' water heaters were installed. Henry used to answer the phone himself and was only later persuaded to have an appointment system and employ a receptionist. Kenneth's salary was not very good, and it soon became clear that the promotion to being a partner was a very distant prospect. Another baby (my nephew, Philip) was on the way and Kenneth was frustrated at being held back in terms of income and responsibility. One day, while they were having coffee after the morning surgery, Kenneth tried to bring him to the point.

About this partnership, he said boldly. Can we fix a date, Henry?

A date? What exactly do you mean, Kenneth?

Well, I've been here two years now and I'd like to know when I'm going to become partner so I can plan for the future.

Henry frowned in concentration and put down his cup. You see, Kenneth, it's not so simple. There's David to consider. (David was his younger son.) If he should want to join the practice I would have to give him first opportunity. He is my son. You understand that.

But David isn't interested in general practice. He wants to be a specialist!

I don't think he's really made up his mind, Kenneth. I do appreciate your position but you must wait a little longer until things become clarified. And if the practice grows, who knows, there may be room for two more partners. But you must be patient.

Kenneth got up with a sigh and left the room. Henry shook his head sadly and poured himself some more coffee.

What can I do? Kenneth said to his father on the phone that evening. He made me a promise but he just wriggles out of it, using David as his excuse. I've worked hard in the practice, I've brought it up to date and made lots of improvements. I think it's time I had a partnership and I'm sure David isn't really interested. Manny discussed it with Florrie in their kitchen. I was upstairs doing my homework.

Was Kenneth very upset? asks Florrie.

Yes he was. He's not getting a fair deal, it seems to me.

What we can do?

Well, he is your cousin? Could you talk to him?

Oh, you know what he's like, Manny. He wouldn't take any notice of me. And I don't know anything about business. You're a man and you're his father. You could go and talk to Henry.

Manny considers this idea for a few moments. All right. If you think that would be best. I'll write to him and go and see him.

On the evening before he is due to go to London, they talk together in bed.

You'll have to be firm with him, Manny.

I'll tell him he can't treat our boy like that.

But you won't be rude to him, will you?

No I won't be rude.

In Willesden, Henry opens the front door of his large corner house and genially welcomes his cousin by marriage. Good to see you, Manny! How is Florrie? A pity she couldn't have come as well. Come in and sit you down. Would you like a cup of tea? Or a whisky?

Manny accepts tea and they sit in Dr Rostov's comfortable lounge.

(Where is Kenneth? Perhaps he is over at the surgery seeing the patients).

How do you find Kenneth? Manny enquires. Are you satisfied with his work?

More than satisfied. He's an excellent young doctor and the patients all like him.

I'm pleased to hear it. But he needs to get himself established. He has a wife and two children to keep. He needs a partnership. Are you still keeping it open for your younger son?

Harry reflects for a moment. Not really... I doubt that he will want to join me now. Although it's always possible.

Then I think it would be best if you offered Kenneth a partnership now, says Manny boldly. Otherwise you'll find that he leaves you. Someone else might jump at the chance of taking him on as a partner. (Nice one, Dad.)

I'll discuss it with Kenneth, says Henry. Of course I want him to stay. I'm sure we can come to an agreement. Why don't the three of us talk about it this evening?

I'm quite proud of my Dad's ability to negotiate, using just a veiled threat at the appropriate moment to make Henry realise that he might be unwise to put off the partnership any longer. Would Kenneth have been able to get another job easily? We don't know. It didn't matter because three months later he was a profit-sharing partner with a contract, his own list of patients and a stake in the practice, which he eventually inherited when Henry retired.

꙳

I should mention that Kenneth was deeply interested in the inner lives of his patients and after a few years, he began to train as a psychoanalyst. The training course at the Institute of Psychoanalysis is long and arduous. To start with, you have to have a personal analysis, five times a week for several years. After two years, you take on a patient, five times a week, with supervision sessions once a week. A year later, a second patient is added. And concurrently there is a programme of lectures and seminars with lots of background reading. Kenneth somehow managed to do this while working full time in the London practice. He did it because his commitment to psychoanalysis burned with a white-hot flame. The revelations about his own unconscious processes and those of his patients constantly amazed him. The power of the ideas to make sense of one's emotional upheavals was inspiring. Michael and I were interested too but never wholly convinced. Was Kenneth's determination to be a follower of Freud a result of Florrie's experience of the treatment at first hand and the presence in our house of books on the subject? After he qualified as an analyst, he continued to practice as a GP as well until he was 60, and wrote several books about how illuminating it was to look at his GP patients through an analytic lens.

Chapter 21
Florrie and Joan

When Florrie was in the early stages of pregnancy with me (we are going back a few years, but not for long) she was contacted by a woman who wanted some advice. Joan was 34 and it was her first pregnancy. She was very apprehensive about how she would cope with the delivery and the responsibility of looking after a tiny baby. Hilda, the maternity nurse, had recommended her to talk to Florrie who, of course, had been through it all twice before. Florrie was pleased to act as a mentor and helper and the two became lifelong friends. Joan had swept-back fair hair and blue eyes. She had a light but resonant voice and always seemed to me to be fastidious and refined. She appeared to float through life in a slightly elevated way. She always had a sleep in the afternoon which was unusual with the rest of Florrie's friends and she seemed to wake enviably refreshed. She was a great cook who could make the most delicious meringues.

Her husband, Joe, was quite different. He was an energetic businessman and solicitor with a teasing sense of humour. If Joan's voice was soft and gentle, Joe's could be loud and challenging. He always seemed happy to talk to me and would ask me questions about school and about my opinions. Of course he had strong views of his own. In spite of being a successful entrepreneur in several different fields including property development and cinema management, he always told me that he was a communist (he had visited Russia several times) and that as soon as the revolution came he would gladly give up his high standard of living and be the same as everyone else. But not until then.

I thought he was teasing but he was probably quite serious, despite the twinkle in his eye.

Meanwhile, until the revolution came, Joe and Joan lived in a large Art Deco style 1930s house which Joe had designed. It had a flat roof and two large sitting rooms, much larger than ours. Strangely, it seemed to have no main door, the usual access being via a kitchen porch which was at the front of the house. There was a double entrance drive so that cars could sweep in at one gate and out through the other. At the back was a large, magnificent garden. It had bedrooms and a bathroom, like any house, but in several respects it was different from any other house I had seen. Firstly, there was a study, leading off the main rear sitting room, in which Joe could ruminate undisturbed over his paperwork. Then there was central heating, previously unknown in Leeds. Finally, upstairs, there was a billiard room with a full sized table.

Florrie was pleased to be asked for her advice on getting through pregnancy and labour. The two babies were due to be born within three months of each other (Florrie's first, then Joan's) so the timing was perfect. They would meet at least once a week at one another's houses for tea and a chat, or for lunch. They discussed food, clothes, friends, and of course, pregnancy. Florrie found that Joan was unusually nervous about the whole process. Although Florrie was prone to anxiety herself, as we know, she was able to forget her own concerns in the process of reassuring Joan.

The two women's abdomens began to bud in parallel. They felt those strange internal kicks together. They could smile and, in privacy, feel in each other's tummies the restless ripples of their babies' limbs. But when they reached their last few weeks, Joan's fragile self-confidence seemed to crack.

I don't think I can go through with this, Florrie. I mean the labour. I don't know how I'm going to be able to do it. To get – you know – the baby through, through *there.*

Listen, said Florrie. What I used to tell myself is this. You're an intelligent person, Florrie. Plenty of women stupider that you have had babies. You can see them all around you. So you can certainly do it too.

But I don't see how it can happen without tearing you apart...

Well, it didn't tear me apart, did it? The thing is, the human body is so adaptable. Your womb and your vagina (as an ex-medical student she felt quite unselfconscious using these words) they can stretch to an amazing degree. Have you ever seen a calf or a lamb being born? (Joan hadn't).

When I was a girl my Dad used to take us on these farm holidays where we used to help out with the animals and saw all these things happening. You realise what a natural process it is.

But the pain must be terrible, Florrie.

No it's not. They give you some gas and air to breathe, chloroform if you need it. You have to push hard, but Sally will be there to hold your hand and get you through it. (Sally was the midwife whom they had in common.)

I was born first. As Florrie was multiparous and I didn't want to give any trouble, we had a short easy labour and delivery. Joan came round to visit and was relieved to see that Florrie looked unharmed by the process. She admired the baby (now happily breastfeeding) and felt that perhaps it was possible to give birth and survive, after all.

Three months later, she too went into labour and was looked after at home by Sally the midwife. Her labour was longer and the delivery more painful than Florrie's but not as bad as she had feared. Her baby was a girl. She was named Marion and it was noticed that we both had a brown mole on our right cheek. (Marion's would later be removed by a dermatologist. I still have mine.) Florrie was able to visit soon after the birth and help her friend to establish breast-feeding. They were soon wheeling their prams together between Sandhill Oval and Alwoodley Lane where the houses were fewer and grander and there was a farm across the road.

Marion and I grew up to be great friends. She was my girl-next-door, always there for me when I needed someone to play with or confide in. Although we didn't actually live next door, her house was only ten minutes walk away and I was always welcomed by Marion and both parents. (They never had any other children.) Usually I went to her house, because my relations with Florrie were in a fractious phase and I needed to get away. Perhaps I am aged somewhere between seven and twelve in this period. So we would play in her house or garden; go for walks across the fields; visit a farm and watch the cows being milked, or ride somewhere in the country on our bikes.

There were family outings too, in Joe's car. We felt less patronised in his car than in Grandpa Jacob's. The attractive little towns of Harrogate and Ilkley were within easy reach. So was Knaresborough, with its river spanned by a dizzying viaduct. At the top of the hill was a mysterious ruined castle with dungeons; and down river was Mother Shipton's Cave, home of the ancient witch who had prophesied the end of the world when Knaresborough Bridge would collapse for the third time. As the castle guide pointed out, it had already fallen twice so the end of the world was a serious possibility. If you're going that way, he would say, *be very careful.*

We also had longer excursions into the Dales. There seemed to be a lot of driving with only short walks when we stopped in a village or went to visit the Aysgarth Falls. But Marion and I enjoyed these trips and so did Florrie. She was not often able to leave her housework and shopping for a day and be driven out into the remote, and in good weather beautiful, scenery of Wharfedale and Wensleydale. She could breathe the fresh air, stop thinking about her responsibilities and enjoy talking to her friend. Joe was always affable, gregarious and outgoing. You didn't have to make an effort with him, because he was so spontaneous and cheerful. What did Manny think about these family outings? He was always quiet. He didn't seem to go in for friends very much. He would talk a bit about business with Joe but he really wasn't in the same league. He was just his quiet self, enjoying the country and pleased that Florrie was happy.

Our most memorable Dales excursion was on June 1ˢᵗ 1953.We drove all the way up gentle Wensleydale, enjoying its quiet winding road, accompanied by a bubbling river and guarded by a Pennine ridge on either side. The journey is punctuated by village greens, duck ponds, farmhouses and fields with sheep and lambs. We stop at Aysgarth to visit the Falls, then on to Bainbridge (village green with stocks) where we have our picnic. As we approach the dale head, the hills become steeper and the valley narrower. The trees disappear and the scenery gets more austere. We reach Hawes where Wensleydale Cheese is made. We visit the Creamery, and Joan and Florrie each buy some to take home. Then, really exciting, Joe drives us up Buttertubs Pass, the famously steep and scary route up to the top of the ridge where there is only bare, bleak moorland with a few sheep staring curiously and misty views of distant hills. Then down with relief into narrower Swaledale. And a long, sleepy journey home.

Back in Alwoodley Lane, Joan provides supper and we sit round their new television watching Eric Robinson's 'Music for You'. The leading guest artist is the legendary tenor Beniamino Gigli, much admired by Joe who can tell us all his history.

The next day, we are back again at their house because it's Coronation Day 1953. The young Queen Elizabeth is to be crowned and not many people have television sets yet. Joan and Joe's is a large screen model but in 1953 that meant only 12 inches wide. And of course it was in black and white, with a picture made up of 405 horizontal lines. But we didn't know any better. We clustered happily round, eating snacks, chatting away and watching the distinguished guests arriving and being pointed out by the awed voice of Richard Dimbleby. Marion and I became restless from time to time and would go up to the billiard room for a game of snooker. But we came back for the central ceremonies of anointing and crowning and so on. My parents and I stayed till about 10 pm when Joe gave us a ride home.

I have no doubt that, as we got into adolescence, our parents hoped that the relationship between Marion and I would turn romantic and that their two babies would eventually fall in love and get married. It didn't happen, but we remained friends with a shared childhood which was important to both of us. She married a young man called David and they had a daughter, Maxine. Tragically, David was killed in an accident when a careless driver collided with his car at night on an icy, wintry road. Maxine was about 16. Marion's mother Joan had died of cancer only a few months earlier and her father a few years before that. Marion sold her marital home and she and Maxine moved back into the art deco mansion in Alwoodley Lane. It seemed to give her the security that she badly needed.

After I left home, we lost contact for a few years until I started to make regular visits to Leeds to see Florrie in her old age.

Chapter 22
Late middle age

In this chapter I am going to look at the years from 1954 to 1965. It's a difficult period for me as storyteller because, although I was alive, and in a position to be observing my mother's late middle age, I was preoccupied with school in the 50s and enjoying my university experience away from home in the early 60s. My brothers were both in different parts of the country (Hull and London), though we did see them and their families from time to time.

Politically, we saw Churchill ceding prime-ministerial power to debonair Anthony Eden who then made a mess of things with Suez and retired to nurse a sick gall bladder. Events, dear boy, said his successor, Harold Macmillan, who proceeded to lead us all into the sunlit uplands of conservative prosperity and national contentment. This lasted until 1963 when sexual intercourse began. John Profumo had an affair with Christine Keeler and lied about it to the House of Commons. Macmillan looked around himself and saw decay and sleaze everywhere. His prostate began to complain and he decided it was time to go. Harold Wilson brought Labour back to power having reforged them in the white heat of technology. Meanwhile popular music changed for ever with the arrival of Bill Haley, Buddy Holly and Elvis.

So what were Florrie and Manny doing in those years of their 50s and 60s? Manny continued to go to Dewsbury on the two buses, with his parcel under his arm. Florrie kept the house clean and did the shopping. She had regular bridge evenings with her women friends. She spent time with Joan. Manny's social life, apart from lunch in Dewsbury with his business cronies, consisted of playing a minor role in Florrie's activities while keeping a watchful eye on the state of her emotions. When bridge was played at home, he greeted the ladies and then retired to the kitchen with a paper or a book and his cigarettes. I was so used to him smoking that I thought nothing about it, until he developed pneumonia and was ill in bed for over a week, having penicillin injections. After that he never smoked again and became rather intolerant of smokers. Fortunately, none of the bridge ladies smoked. Manny would join them after the game for tea and buns or perhaps one of Florrie's much admired, feather-light sponge cakes with jam and cream.

In 1954, Grandpa Jacob developed cancer of the colon and had to have a colostomy. By this time he had remarried, and although his second wife, Mary, and Florrie were never really friends, they remained polite to each other. We continued to go round to their house on occasional Saturdays, but not every week. Sometimes I was able to play with my step-cousin Tim who had come to visit his grandmother. Then poor Jacob went into hospital and Florrie visited him there. When he came home he seemed to be a stricken old man, disgusted with the way his bowel had let him down, after a lifetime of being in control. Florrie had sadly watched him go down hill and had become accustomed to the idea that he would die. This time she felt supported by all three of her brothers as, in the by-now expected squabbles over the will, his children were all content with their inheritance but combined to express resentment against his widow. Poor lady, she must have been grieving too, but none of the conversations I overheard at home had any sympathy for her. So we must say goodbye to Jacob, the indomitable, Churchillian battler, godfather and founder of the Rostov dynasty. Did he break my mother's heart with his contempt for her marriage?

Why couldn't Rachel intervene? I can't tell, because I only see them on a flickering black and white screen with indistinct sound. Jacob's younger brother Isaac outlived him by 14 years, although his own wife, Annie, died, the year after Jacob.

By this time I was well established at the Grammar School and like my father, taking two bus rides to get to my work each morning. The rough, often brutal Grammar School culture was quite different from that of Miss Rider's gentle preparatory school. For one thing it was all male (apart from a couple of fierce hair-pulling female teachers in charge of the junior forms). Like many others of its day, it was modelled on the Public Schools with lots of appeals to playing the game and being proud of being British. There was a constant threat of violence from the masters, many of whom were eccentric and unpredictable of mood. At least two seemed to be quite unhinged. Most of them regarded corporal punishment as an integral part of their vocation, but they didn't bother to buy canes. They armed themselves with a variety of lengths of wood with which they would 'whack' the boys' bottoms for the slightest infringement of discipline. Or lack of effort. With some masters, it was possible to relax, knowing that you were not in danger unless you did anything really bad (which I never did). With others you had to be constantly on your guard. The merest hint of dumb insolence could trigger a summary beating in front of the class.

Thank goodness this sort of reign of terror is no longer tolerated in the name of education. I never mentioned anything about it at home and I don't think my parents ever realised what went on. I was only occasionally beaten myself, but there was the constant threat that it might happen if I wasn't careful. At times I wondered whether the Grammar was really a 'better' school than the state grammar school my elder brothers went to. Why did my parents want to send me to a posh school? They had to pay quite a lot in fees for the first two years until I won a scholarship which paid for everything.

However, I didn't spend all my middle school years in anxious vigilance, as I believe the child protection experts call it. I made some friends. I was no good at games but fortunately the school regarded music as a competitive sport. By the time I got to the fifth form and was studying for my O levels (now GCSE) the atmosphere was more relaxed, and we seemed, thank goodness, too grown up to be hit with sticks of wood.

During these years I was getting interested in music. Florrie had got me started on the piano at the age of seven, but I never really took to it and was allowed to stop. Big mistake. Florrie, why didn't you make me go on, or use some of the subtle tactics that Grandma Rachel used on you to make you continue? You must have decided that children shouldn't be coerced into doing things they hated. And yet, if you had persisted, if I had persisted, I might by now be stumble through a Chopin Waltz or a Mozart sonata. I might have been one of those people who can just sit down and play anything you like, like Sam in *Casablanca*. Perhaps not. Happily, Kenneth got me interested in the recorder, and I went on from there to the clarinet which Uncle Harry bought me as a present for my 13ᵗʰ birthday. I remember sitting up I bed and fondling its wonderful gleaming silver keys and coaxing a few lower register notes out of its thick black cylindrical tube. I was eventually able to play the Mozart and Brahms quintets with amateur string quartets. That must be counted as one of my greatest pleasures. So Grandma Rachel's musical influence did come through to me and find expression in the end. But I still can't read the bass clef.

In 1956, after a series of miscarriages, Pat and Michael had their first baby, Valerie. She was followed, in the ensuing year by Paul. (Valerie became a professor of English literature at Hull University and Paul a consultant physician.) Florrie and Manny had two new grandchildren, not so far away, and we would visit them at weekends. I enjoyed talking to Michael about being a doctor, and going round on house calls with him.

When it came to choosing my A level subjects, the headmaster of the Grammar School told me I should do classics. But I want to be a doctor, I protested. I should be doing science. The headmaster waved this objection aside. Doing classics will give you a broad education, he said. You can easily do medicine after that. And I suppose he was right. I just wanted to get on with being a doctor and not have to spend more time learning Latin and Greek. Our progress was so slow in these subjects that, even after three years I was still unaware of the delights of reading classical literature in the original. In any case, I suspected that the Head was chiefly anxious to keep its shrinking classical studies department going. And to win Oxbridge Scholarships for the glory of the school. These prizes too were dangled, spinning, before my eyes.

When I reported this to my parents, they didn't really know what I was talking about. We had a perfectly good university and medical school in our own city which had served Michael and Kenneth very well. Oxford and Cambridge were semi-mythical places attended by aristocratic young men in novels such as *Brideshead Revisited.* Their only reality seemed to be as competitors in the annual University Boat Race. Then Florrie recalled that Theresa Raisman, the daughter of her close friend Ray, had been to Oxford on a scholarship and got a first class degree. So it was possible for ordinary mortals and the grandchildren of immigrants.

I didn't get a scholarship but I did manage to scrape an entrance to one of the Oxford colleges which welcomed me very kindly. My father measured me for new suits (he made all my outer clothes) including a dinner jacket which I still occasionally wear, never having bought another. It's nice to look at the inside pocket and see the label: E Levinsky, Tailor and Costumier. It's my last personal link with him as a tailor. To these and all my shirts, pyjamas and underwear, my mother stitched Cash's nametapes so that I wouldn't lose them. She packed everything in an old cabin trunk that had belonged to Grandpa Jacob and still bore the torn, faded labels of shipping companies. He had used it on his business trips to America on the Queen Mary in the 1930s. The trunk was dispatched ahead of me by British Railways' 'Passenger Luggage in Advance' service. Three days later I set off myself, with a small suitcase containing some clothes and books, some emergency food rations added by my mother and one luxury item: a tin of homemade meringues from Auntie Joan, Marion's mother.

My parents both stood in the drive, waving goodbye, as the taxi came to took me to the station. Manny's face was creased and resolute. Florrie looked bravely encouraging. Were they sad to see me go? Their last chick leaving the nest? I remember finding Florrie shedding tears as she cleaned the cooker one day, shortly after Michael and Pat went off to Hull. Kenneth had already gone to do his National Service. I asked why she was crying, and she explained, smiling through the tears that it made her feel sad that two of her children had grown up and would be with her no more and that she was missing them. Then she wiped her eyes and went on with cleaning.

Now there would just be the two of them, as they had been before we were born. Of course they would see us every few months, but it wouldn't be the same as having children tumbling about the place and coming for a cuddle when they needed one.

I feel their nostalgia for our childhood and am comforted by the thought that, despite all the conflicts in their early years together and the painful quarrels that I had overheard as a child, despite all that, they would look after each other. They had a print of a picture by Pissarro called *The Road to Louveciennes* over the mantelpiece in the dining room. Maybe they bought it on our holiday in Paris. It showed a long, tree-lined street with a middle aged or elderly couple, outlined in a few dabs of paint, clinging together as they walked along. My brothers and I all thought that the couple in the picture were Florrie and Manny. Years later, when the picture had disappeared along with most of Florrie's personal effects, I caught sight of the original painting in an alcove, high up on the top floor of the *Musée d'Orsay* in Paris. No one else had scaled the stairs to reach this highest tower of the old train station. I sat, gazing at it for half an hour, happily reunited with the picture that had been at the centre of my parents' home and mine.

I soon became totally involved in being a student and didn't think about my parents very much. I wrote home every two weeks, including lists of my expenditure to show that I was spending my allowance only on necessities and small occasional treats. These were precise to the nearest halfpenny and I think they both found them amusing. Occasionally I would request extra money, which was generally forthcoming. I would be back with then in the vacations, but spending time with my Leeds friends, I didn't give much thought to them.

In my last term at Oxford I met and fell in love with Mary, who was in her first term. After that I moved to London to do clinical medicine at St Mary's Hospital but we continued to see each other every other weekend. In one of my regular letters to my parents I disclosed that we were planning to get married. I knew this would be a shock, because she was not one of our people. She and her mother were serious members of the Church of England and her late father had been a Catholic. Marrying out of the faith was regarded as a major blow by our people, even those like Florrie and Manny who were not particularly religious. Only one Levinsky (my Uncle Eli) had ever married out and no Rostovs had ever crossed this particular line. I seem to have set a precedent, however, because ever since I married out, no one of our family has married in. In the early part of the last century some fundamentalist parents had been know to react in an extreme way, cutting off the offending son or daughter and behaving as if they had never existed. How they managed this absurd denial I have no idea. Florrie and Manny would be disturbed, I reasoned, possibly upset and angry, but in time they would come round. But Manny, the guardian of Florrie's emotional stability, was very concerned that such a marriage might tip her over into another breakdown. Even before the news of my 'engagement' she had already been having some more therapy with Dr Guntrip about which I knew nothing.

My brothers decided that they should intervene to protect our mother from any reckless action on my part. We all met in a hotel in London where Michael and Pat were staying. My big brothers broke the news to me that our mother had been in fragile emotional health for most of her life and had been having therapy on and off for years. This was the first I had heard of her being ill enough to need treatment, though of course I was well aware of her periods of depression and her angry scolding. I didn't know that there was also a problem with compulsive rituals, although I knew all about the perfectionism, and repetitive cleaning and bed making. It all made sense. What didn't make sense was that my happiness with Mary could make Florrie worse or precipitate a disaster. So I held firm, agreeing only that we wouldn't get married until after I had qualified as a doctor. I would become an apostate but not a married man with no means of support, which would have been an even greater cause of distress to Florrie.

In the event, Mary was accepted without much difficulty. She got on well with both Manny and Florrie and there were no conflicts of the rather pointless kind that broke out from time to time with their other daughters-in-law. Possibly Mary's otherness and loyalty to a different religion created a kind of protective distance which everyone respected. Perhaps they saw that we were happy together and realised that that was good fortune enough and that they were too old to try to mould the life of their youngest child in the traditional pattern. We were married within a few weeks of my passing my final exams in medicine.

Our wedding was a small-scale secular affair conducted in the Oxford Register Office and followed by a lunch in a restaurant. Florrie and Manny came with Kenneth and Nettie and Michael (Pat was recovering from a miscarriage). Mary's family were represented by her mother, her godfather, Ivor Bulmer-Thomas, and a family friend, Mr Ziman, known as 'Z'. Like Mary and her mother, the two men were upper middle class, Oxbridge educated Englishers who spoke in a refined way without any regional accent. Manny established that Z was of Jewish origin, although he had long severed any connection with our people. He was an interesting man who wrote leading articles for *The Times*. When the lunch was over (there were no speeches) Manny accidentally went off wearing Z's overcoat. The coats were later exchanged with some slight embarrassment. I found this incident intriguing. Had my father been unconsciously trying to slip on a more 'English' identity in the form of a coat, his own stock-in-trade? Perhaps he was imagining himself as a Jew transformed into a perfect Englisher.

As Mary was about to get into the taxi to the airport to begin our honeymoon (in Paris) Florrie took Mary by the hand and whispered: *take care of him*. Mary said that she would. And so my mother handed me over. She survived my marrying-out without any adverse effects on her mental health. She continued to get on well with Mary, even comparing her to Ruth, the biblical daughter-in-law from outside the faith. Mary liked her too, although she never felt quite at ease amid the alien corn.

Chapter 23
An old couple

After our wedding, Mary and I plunged into creating our own adult life as a couple. We lived in or near London while I worked as a junior doctor in various hospitals. I phoned 'home' to speak to them about once a week and we paid occasional visits to Leeds. But I thought very little about them on the whole. They had a life of their own in which I took probably as little interest as my own grown up children now take in mine. She was in her mid sixties, he in his mid seventies. During this time Manny gradually allowed his tailoring business to run down until finally, in 1968, he stopped going to Dewsbury altogether. But a good income continued to flow in from the rental of the premises to Wigfalls, who now sold more television sets than radios. Florrie continued to do housework, assisted by a series of 'daily helps'. Many of the tasks which fed her obsessional tendencies had now thankfully gone. Cutlery no longer had to be cleaned; there was a washing machine and obviously much less washing to do. She continued to shop and cook, to meet her friends for bridge games and to visit and be visited by her brothers and their wives. These now included Harry's second wife, Betty, a cheerful, energetic, sporty woman who called her 'Florence', was clearly fond of her and seemed to have a tonic effect on her. They both took up painting in oils in the open air. One of their favourite subjects was the ruined Norman Abbey at Kirkstall. Betty's paintings were competent but conventional. But Florrie found that she could use the palette knife to plaster on thick layers of green, brown and stone grey which evoked the solid character of the old stones in their setting of earth and trees.

Florrie and Manny had a holiday on their own in France and a trip to Israel, after the 1967 war made Jerusalem more accessible. Here they met a number of Rostov relatives who had escaped the Holocaust. They must have been descendants of Jacob's cousins from the *shtetls* in the old empire of the Czar. I listened politely to their traveller's tales but at that time I really wasn't very interested and the visit was never repeated. They started going to the south-west for regular holidays: to Torquay, and later to Falmouth in Cornwall.

Kenneth and Nettie had two more boys in the mid 1960s (Stephen and Simon) and Michael and Pat had a younger daughter (Rosemary). Florrie enjoyed the company of her grandchildren and they loved coming to visit her and playing with my old toys which were kept for them under the bed in the spare room. Jeremy, Kenneth and Nettie's eldest, came to Leeds University and would often go round to his grandparents for a meal or some advice and support.

Financially, Michael was now comfortably off though working very hard. Kenneth and I were still short of money, especially for housing. Kenneth was now a partner in the London Rostov practice, but he was paying for his own training in psychoanalysis. Neither of us had any inhibitions about asking our father for money and he generally responded but we never got quite as much as we wanted.

This was because Manny didn't have it to spare without calling on Florrie's reserves which she wanted to keep for the rainy day that might come again. Kenneth needed a deposit for a new house but was only offered an insufficient amount, which he refused. Somehow he found the money in the end and the house increased in value rapidly in the property boom of the early 1970s. I asked for and received a small subsidy towards the rent of our flat in the little dormitory town of Egham (Surrey) which was convenient for the hospital.

Although I originally wanted to be a GP like my brothers, I became more interested in hospital medicine and was hoping to become a consultant physician. But this was very competitive. I passed the exams (at the third attempt) and gained plenty of clinical experience. But the next stage was to do research, involving trials of new treatments on severely ill patients. I found the negotiation and the lack of transparency with the 'volunteers' uncomfortable, and I struggled with the maths and statistics involved. I began to think it would be wiser to give up and be a GP after all. I discussed the problem with Michael who at first urged me to press on with my hospital ambition, as I might otherwise 'always regret it'. I guess he still had some of that regret himself. But by 1972, after a total lack of progress with research and a number of failed attempts to get a post at a more senior level, I gave up and opted for general practice. I felt I would be happier working with people than with abstract science; I would be financially better off and I could stay in London. Aspiring consultants had to be content to go anywhere in the country where a suitable job was offered. I wrote my father a letter telling him of my decision He told Michael who wrote me a letter telling me I was doing the right thing and general practice was a wonderful career.

I think he was right the second time and I have never regretted the decision. I worked with Kenneth as a trainee assistant for six months (Dr Rostov had by this time retired) and then found a partnership vacancy in north-west London where I remain to this day. What did Florrie think about my career plans? I don't know if she was sorry not to have a son who was a consultant. The idea persisted that 'specialists' were superior to family doctors, intellectually and socially. But not many families had one, and I think she was just relieved to see me 'settled'.

The fact that we had all become doctors must have been a source of satisfaction to Florrie. Did she think: They wouldn't let me train as a doctor, so I produced three doctors of my own. If so, she kept such thoughts to herself and always gave the impression that she never wanted to do medicine all that much, it was her father's idea. But that year as a student had been very special. It was a glimpse into a wider world where women did things and made things happen outside the family and the home. A world she might have been part of.

But all that was long in the past, as were the conflicts with her father and brothers. By this time she and Manny had completed the more difficult tasks of their marriage and they were still together. They were still fond of each other and they understood each other better.

In the autumn of 1972 they celebrated their Golden Wedding with a party at the Astoria, a reception hall in the older part of Leeds. This was a grand occasion. Both my brothers were there with their wives and children. All three of my Rostov uncles, now in their sixties, came with their wives and their children. There were even some of the rarely seen Levinsky relatives including Uncle Julius, Manny's eldest brother, and Aunt Laura who had introduced her brother to Florrie. By this time,

Mary and I had a seven-month-old baby (Tom) who attracted lots of admiration to the satisfaction of his parents. Florrie looked happy and regal, as she nearly always did on public occasions.

In the spring of 1974 we had another baby (a little girl called Kate) and I have a photograph of my father holding her in the garden of the house in Sandhill Oval. I was glad this was taken as he died in June of the same year.

He had begun to have angina (chest pain due to coronary artery disease) and had seen the doctor. Then my mother telephoned to say that he had been very unwell and had been admitted to hospital. Two days later I had a distressed call from her to say that he was getting worse and the hospital doctors had told her to 'send for her sons'.

I excused myself from a practice meeting and drove the 200 miles to Leeds. When I arrived at the house I was met by Auntie Ada, who gave me a hug and wished me 'a long life'. This is what our people say to someone who has just been bereaved, so I knew that I had arrived too late to see my Dad again. Eventually, my mother and Kenneth and Uncle Benny arrived at the house and there was much discussion about the funeral, in which I took no part. Florrie seemed to be numb, as one might expect. I went to bed in my old room and read a diary of my father's that I found in his dressing table drawer. It was a small black book in which he had made multiple short entries on the same day in successive years, so it was sometimes hard to know in which year anything had happened. I could see that, in the last few years, Florrie had again been depressed and spending too much time on repetitive obsessional activities. He records how she had gone back into treatment with Harry Guntrip who was now quite elderly (he died in 1975). Florrie's progress seems to be slow or non-existent, making Manny anxious. How much longer is this going on? He wonders, in one entry. And then: Decided to go and see Guntrip myself. A few days later: Guntrip says psychoanalysis is a slow process. Things may get worse before they get better.

When we get to June, the entries begin to thin out. Getting chest pain again. Tablets help but it comes on again if I walk too fast. Next day: angina getting worse. Seeing doctor tomorrow. That was the final entry. On the next day he was admitted to hospital.

The funeral was my first. It took place at the old cemetery on the edge of the city, that our people started when the first community was established. There was a brief service in a tiny chapel resembling a Gothic garden shed. The rabbi gave a short and apt eulogy. Manny had been a quiet, modest man, he said, who was genuinely interested in what people had to say. A good husband and father. We then processed, following the coffin through the ranks of stones, marking the graves of everyone in the community who had died before him, arranged, as I have said previously, in chronological order, until we reached the raw edge with a green field space waiting for further burials. The coffin was a plain wooden box, pushed to the graveside on a little trolley. As it was lowered into the grave, I held Florrie's arm and whispered that it wasn't really Daddy any more, he was somewhere else. I now know that this was to comfort myself. The tradition is not to disguise the bleakness and the finality; the fact that we depart from the world with nothing, just as we came in. The mourners themselves are expected to pick up the spades provided and shovel the heavy clay soil of Leeds on to the coffin. The clods of earth clatter harshly. The coffin is gradually covered. Then the professional gravediggers finish off. We three sons recited, in unison, the ancient Kaddish prayer of farewell to a parent. Michael knew the Hebrew words well, but Kenneth and I had to struggle. Afterwards, many people came up to shake our hands and wish us a long life. Back at the house, it was hard to believe that Manny had really gone forever. I felt that he might still be sitting quietly in the next room reading his paper. Florrie said she kept wanting to tell him things. Kenneth saw a rabbit in the back garden and thought it might be him, watching us. Nobody cried very much. I didn't cry at all until I was driving back to London the next day when grief suddenly caught me and I had to stop in a lay-by and let myself go.

Chapter 24
Living alone

Florrie now began a long period of living on her own at the house in Sandhill Oval. She was 73 when Manny died and still in good physical health. I began to visit her about every three months to begin with, and then more often. A year after the funeral, we had the ceremony of setting the stone on Manny's grave. This was like a shadowy repeat of the funeral, with all the relatives gathered as before, but just a few prayers. The stone was already in place and beside it was a vacant plot ready for Florrie. I continued to be gloomily fascinated by this cemetery with its regular ranks of gravestones in chronological order. Those who had died in the last year (and were not yet ready to have their stones put up) occupied the last row, after which a green field stretched away to a perimeter wall. Beyond this was another empty field. I tried to calculate where my plot would be, assuming I lived a reasonable span and was somehow gathered back into the community after my death. This was and is unlikely to happen, but I was surprised to find that I quite liked entertaining the idea.

Sometimes I visited with Mary and the children. Other times I went by myself for the weekend. We would usually encounter one or more of my uncles, and we fell into a pattern of visiting them at their homes as well. Florrie seemed to have come to terms with being without Manny and was usually cheerful. We never discussed her feelings of loss and I don't know what dark thoughts she had when she was by herself. In 1977 we had a holiday in Bridlington. I had enjoyed it there so much as a child that I wanted to share it with my own children and was gratified to find that it charmed them too. Michael and Pat came over from Hull (not far away) and Florrie came over on the bus for the day, also revisiting her past. She told me for the first time about the family holidays in the 1930s before I was born. Sometimes on London visits she stayed with me, but more often with Kenneth and Nettie. Relations were not always good. She was quick to take offence if she was not invited for a particular meal or she was asked, for practical reasons, when she was planning to return home.

In January 1982, we celebrated Florrie's 80th birthday with a lunch at the Parkway Hotel in Leeds. A little bunch of her old friends were there, including the bridge playing Sclare sisters and Ray Raisman, who used to baby-sit me when my parents went out. We had some fun remembering those evenings. Our children were admired and indulged by the Uncles and Aunts. The next day we visited Uncle Abe, and Kate showed my musical uncle what she could do on the piano. Later on, he played part of a Schubert sonata for me. I went home and started to listen to Schubert's late piano music, as I have done with great pleasure ever since. I am still grateful to him for opening that door for me.

At about this time Florrie started to show signs of failing health. She complained of leg pains which no doctor seemed able to explain or relieve. I think she had osteoarthritis of the lower spine and they were sciatic pains, common enough, but somehow I didn't expect her to have them. She was also more obviously low in spirits and complained of loneliness, although she was visited quite regularly by her brothers. She was invited to supper by Abe and Tess on Friday nights and this soon became a weekly treat.

Although she enjoyed these occasions, everyone noticed that she had become quite deaf and this excluded her from conversations with more than one person, which is what generally happens. But she didn't want to wear a hearing aid. When I asked about this, she would say she didn't want to be seen wearing an aid because people would think she was handicapped and pity her! She wouldn't even have the telephone altered so the volume would be higher. I didn't argue with her. I think I had learned something about how to get on with old people without getting upset and irritated. You need patience, tolerance and a willingness to accept other people's firmly held beliefs. I try to do this with my elderly patients too. I'm not sure whether my insights came from them or from Florrie. It's a pity that other people were not always so patient with her.

On one of her visits to London, I took her to the opera at Covent Garden to see the great Welsh baritone, Geraint Evans, giving one of his farewell performances in Donizetti's *L'elisir d'amore*. Of course, she knew exactly who Geraint Evans was and had seen him on television but never in the theatre. We had good seats at the side of the stalls circle and an excellent view of the stage. I could see that she was alert throughout and clearly enjoying it. I remembered her stories about being taken to the opera in Leeds as a little girl by her mother. Although she may have complained about being dragged along when she was a child, opera became and remained something she loved and was not often able to see live in a theatre. It felt good to be able to take her one more time, probably the last time. It was also a kind of salute to Rachel, my grandmother, across the century.

Florrie's deafness gradually got worse and she found it increasingly difficult to walk. We still managed some short excursions in our local park when she visited. Sometimes, on my visits to Leeds I would take her shopping. As we walked slowly down the County Arcade, Florrie hanging on to my arm, I noticed the Amplivox Hearing Aid Centre. Come in for free consultation and hearing test! It said. To my surprise Florrie agreed to go in. We were greeted by a large, cheerful man with a confidence-inspiring manner, and waved to a couple of chairs in front of his desk.

DO YOU HAVE DIFFICULTY IN HEARING PEOPLE? he asked. Florrie smiled and nodded.

BUT YOU CAN HEAR ME ALL RIGHT? (Florrie nods again. She likes this man).

THAT'S BECAUSE I HAVE A VERY LOUD CLEAR VOICE.

So she let him test her hearing and do an audiogram and explain the benefits of his firm's hearing aids. He recommended an in-the-ear moulded model at £415. He pointed out that this would not only restore her hearing but be INVISIBLE. She listened politely, but, in the end, said she would have to think about it. Later, Uncle Abe told us that National Health Aids were just as good, but he couldn't wear one because a previous operation on his ear had damaged his trigeminal nerve.

That evening she said, I wish you would all come back to Leeds. I could watch my grandchildren growing up and have my daughters-in-law popping in and out.

That was a bit heart-wrenching and I toyed with the prospect briefly; but soon saw that it wouldn't do and that I couldn't bear not to live in London. Instead of her daughters-in-law, she had cousin Jean who came regularly and did shopping for her. Unfortunately this came to and end when they had a 'falling out' over a remark that Florrie made about Jean's mother, which was taken amiss. Over such small but unforgiven misunderstandings, a huge hole can be torn in the social support network for an old person. Jean stopped calling round and no longer did any shopping for Florrie. But Florrie still managed to cook lunch and supper for us. I realised that most of her shopping was now done by cousin Harriet (Peter's wife) who visited regularly and was fortunately much appreciated by Florrie.

In March 1987 I took myself to Leeds on the train. As we reached Leeds, snow was falling quite heavily. We watched an instalment of Ingmar Bergman's film *Fanny and Alexander* on television. Florrie stayed awake and thoroughly engaged.. She said she identified with Alexander and his anger at his mother for marrying again after his father's death. She still remembered her own disturbed feelings, at the age of 52, when her father married again. She was now 85. She felt depressed and neglected by her family. She couldn't hear properly and she had painful unreliable legs. She said we (her sons) should have persuaded her to buy that flat (which was now no longer available). She could be irritating if you let this sort of thing get to you. And yet she could still respond with such warmth of feeling and intelligence to something like the Bergman film. The next day, I cleared a path in the snow, and, with plastic bags wrapped round my shoes, I walked over to Uncle Harry and Auntie Betty's. They were as cordial as ever, but they made sure that I heard their views on Florrie's situation. I think they expected me to do something. They probably did the same to my brothers when they visited. She should have bought that flat, she says, but she only wanted it when it was off the market! She's always on about things she shouldn't have done, they went on. She even says she shouldn't have married your Dad! (I was too dumbfounded to respond to that one.) Back at Sandhill Oval, Florrie was tearful and said that nobody loved her. I gave her a big hug and said that I loved her, anyway. We had tea, and I had to leave her, waving from the front door as I got in my taxi for the station.

On another of my weekend visits, we went shopping for a new television for her. But she didn't like the stark functional designs of that time and preferred to keep her old set which was 'a nice piece of furniture'. The next day (Sunday) she was in a reminiscent mood. She told me about her first love, Jimmy Barclay, from Dewsbury. He was 16 and she was 13 when they met. He gave her a little gold heart as a keepsake when he went off to the First World War. He was killed in action and she never saw him again. She had kept the little heart in her button box for 60 years. I knew that button box well, and, as a child, had often played with the buttons. But when we opened the box and looked for the heart it was no longer there. Then, she remembered that she had looked at it recently, thought unsentimentally, what was the good of keeping things like that – and had thrown it away.

We also talked about her need to sell the shop in Dewsbury. This was the one that caused so much emotional conflict in the 1920s when Grandfather Rostov bought it from the Levinskys and put it in Florrie's name. Wigfalls, the television firm, no longer wanted to rent it, and it had been empty for some months with no prospect of another tenant. The general opinion was that the building would not fetch more than £50,000; Florrie insisted that she wanted £70, 000. She held out and to our surprise, eventually got it.

Later in the summer, we visited my brother Michael and my sister-in-law, Pat in Hull and discussed 'what was to be done' about Florrie. I realised that, living relatively near to Leeds, they came under much more pressure from the Leeds family to persuade her to give up living alone. Distress calls from Florrie herself also came more frequently to Michael, as the eldest son. Pat felt that Michael was being asked to make too many weekend trips to Leeds when he was tired from being on call at night for his patients. She also told us that she had wanted Florrie to treat her like a daughter, and felt hurt when Florrie said 'you can never really feel at home in a daughter-in-law's house'. Pat thinks that we were all brought up without enough warmth and physical affection. Could this be true? I wondered. Certainly we don't go in for much hugging and handholding. But I have always thought of Florrie as warm-hearted and affectionate. Did I get a better deal as a result of being 'the baby'? This may well be so. But I think I had a better understanding that there was no point in expecting her, at her age, to accept rational arguments about the need to give up her house and move into sheltered accommodation.

Sometimes she would subject me to a long recital about how unhappy she was. She was so lonely, her legs were constantly painful and can't be relied on not to give way when she walks. Going out on her own is becoming almost impossible. I found the emotional intensity of this quite hard to bear. It felt as if her distress and bitterness was being loaded onto me and was weighing me down. She also talked about getting a flat in London which was quite unrealistic. However, I managed to accept what she had to unload without getting irritable or arguing. After lunch on Sunday we had a session about the lost flat in Leeds in the block where Harry and Benny and their wives are living.

I should have taken it, she said. Why didn't you persuade me? And then, after a pause in which I said nothing, I don't blame anyone.

In March 1989, my Uncle Harry, eldest of Florrie's brothers, died from a heart attack. He was 85. Again, all three of her sons were at the funeral to support her and say goodbye to Harry. She showed very little emotion and it was difficult to know what she was thinking. I gave Auntie Betty a hug and told Philippa what a wonderful uncle he had been. She seemed surprised!

In April, Florrie came to stay with Kenneth and Nettie and spent time with us too. She grumbled about being 'parcelled out' and told where to go on which days. I ended up quarrelling on the phone with Kenneth about this, as if I was the one feeling offended instead of her. Then tempers were calmed. Everyone settled down. We took her to Kenwood House where she enjoyed looking at the pictures and pointed out several things I hadn't observed, mainly to do with brushstrokes and the painting of lace and drapery. She listened to Kate playing the piano and we took her out for a successful Chinese meal.

During the next two years (1990-91) Florrie's unsteadiness on her feet relentlessly worsened. She could navigate herself round her house only by hanging on to familiar chairs and tables. She was like the captain of her ship, walking the deck with heaving seas and a force nine gale blowing. A fall seemed inevitable before long. She now had a home help, meals on wheels and two Zimmer frames (one for upstairs). I don't know how she managed to get up and down those stairs by herself. She had decided not to come and stay with us over Christmas 1991 and we were all aware that January 20th 1992 would be her ninetieth birthday. Michael had arranged a slightly early celebration for her about which she had mixed feelings, but in the end it was a success. Again, some of her old friends turned up, sadly looking rather decrepit, as well as relatives from both sides of the family. Florrie made a smiling, royal entrance, and enjoyed receiving everyone's love and congratulations. Her good humour continued through to the next day.

She survived through 1992 despite a succession of nosebleeds one of which required an admission to hospital. In March 1993, I visited with Kate who wanted to record an interview with Florrie for a university project on education. I have the tape still and it is nice to hear my Mum's voice. Her account of her schooldays (from the age of three) is coherent and thoughtful and sparkles with humour. She sums up her brief time at Leeds University as 'one of the best years of my life.' What she loved was the chance to mix with and talk to all the other bright young people, especially the more mature students who were returning from the war after the Armistice. It becomes clear to me when I listen to the tape again, that her commitment to medicine was never very deep. She was only sixteen when she started at the university and as she says, medicine had been her father's plan for her. If she had been encouraged and enabled to switch to biology, she would probably have completed the course and graduated. She would then have been able to continue taking part in the exhilarating world of ideas which she had tasted so briefly. She would have been able to work outside the home and achieve intellectual independence as well as earning her own money. That this didn't happen is nobody's fault, but it is a pity that she never 'fulfilled her potential'. I think she was more pleased that her sons had graduated than that they had become doctors.

Her brothers were also sadly deprived of all the benefits of higher education. Uncle Abe might well have been a professor of music. But by now he was getting old as well. At about this time he had a second stroke and was sadly unable to speak or to swallow. It was hard and painful trying to communicate with him. But Tess said he was looking forward to watching a television programme about Schoenberg.

ॐ

As Florrie's difficulties at home became worse, my brothers and I began talking about nursing homes. We went to see (without Florrie) a new and quite small old peoples' home about half a mile from the house, near the stop where I waited for the bus to take me to the Grammar School. It was quite a pleasant place, more like a Holiday Inn than an institution, but the rooms were very small. Michael and Pat wanted to persuade her to move in there, and her situation certainly very fragile by this stage. There were so many things she needed: more medical attention, new clothes, more help at home in dressing, cooking, shopping and going out. But as soon as we started talking dates and decisions she would divert onto another problem. A week before Christmas (for which we had been expecting her to come and stay), Michael and Pat visited Florrie and found her in a pathetic and panicky state. She wanted to be taken back to Hull with them but this wasn't possible. So Michael arranged an immediate admission to the little home by the bus stop (Carmel Lodge) where she agreed to stay for a week or two. In the event, it was the end of her independent living. She was nearly 92.

Chapter 25
Final years

The last few years of Florrie's life make a sad story of slow decline. She was marooned in one care home or another, cut off from her family and friends and rapidly losing the ability to do anything for herself. It is a terrible thing not to be able to stand up and walk by yourself any longer. Many old people, if they live long enough, suffer this progressive weakness of the legs combined with loss of the art of balance and the ability to control where your legs are going. Medical explanations are vague and non-specific. The site of the trouble cannot be localised in the brain and the underlying cause is attributed to inadequate cerebral blood supply or 'degenerative' processes. There is no cure and it goes on getting worse. Pain becomes a regular if not a constant companion. But worse than the physical pain is the spiritual pain of someone stuck in a home for the aged. That is if you still have the capacity to think and feel and be aware of your surroundings. You are not only unable to move without the risk of falling, but you are surrounded in your tight little ring of armchairs by a company of ghosts; people whose deterioration has destroyed their memories and their cognitive abilities. The sufferers from dementia. She is not as bad as those others, say your family. But perhaps you are worse off, because you are still awake and acutely aware of your terrible plight. As Long John Silver says, somewhere in *Treasure Island*, 'Them as die will be the lucky ones'. But who knows? Maybe your slumped and drooling companions are inwardly just as aware or have some remnant of awareness and are equally unhappy, although they can't express it. I remember a patient of mine, a proud, indomitable, intellectual old lady called Miss Silver, whom I used to visit at home regularly. When she finally had to go into an elderly care ward in the hospital, I visited her there and had some difficulty in finding her among her demented fellow patients. Some were shaking, some were moaning to themselves and one was calling out for a nurse. Then Miss Silver saw me and raised a hand in an ironic greeting. 'Here we all are, doctor', she said, 'poor suffering humanity'. As a life-long socialist she wanted to cry out on behalf of everyone and not just herself.

But for Florrie, the worst pain was missing her own house. She never intended to stay in Carmel Lodge for more than a fortnight and her thoughts recurred constantly to how she was going to get back home. I felt her separation from the house keenly, as if I shared it. I had been born and brought up at 62 Sandhill Oval and still thought of it as my home too. However, during these years I was able to get closer to my mother. Or perhaps return to the kind of closeness we had enjoyed in our first years together.

After she moved into Carmel Lodge, I began visiting more often, usually about once a month. My brothers also visited regularly but usually our visits were planned not to coincide. My particular contribution, in the first year, was to take her back to her house for the weekend. She was always happy to get away. If I stay here, she said, I'll begin to get like the others. The staff at the home got used to the idea of these excursions and usually had her ready when I arrived. I would help her down the stairs from her room and into the car. Then we would drive the short distance to the house. If it was winter I would have been there first to put the central heating on. I used to bring food with me to make her some lunch. (Yes, after so many years of feeding me, she permitted our roles to be reversed.) Generally I brought food that I knew we would both like and that was simple enough for me to prepare. The usual lunch menu was smoked salmon followed by fish cakes and baked potato with apple pie and ice cream for dessert. After lunch, we might have a little drive to Harrogate and look at a shop or two, if she was up to it. Sometimes we visited my friend Marion, now back in her parents' old house after her husband's death. Florrie, who knew that house well, was interested in the changes that Marion had made. Back in our house, we would have some supper and watch television together. Then, I would help her to get to bed in her old bedroom where she had slept with Manny and where I had been born. And I would sleep in my own bedroom next door. On the Sunday morning, she needed some help getting out of the bath and once had a moment of panic as I tried to help her down the stairs. When it was time for me to drive back to London, I would return her sadly to the penitentiary and promise to visit again soon.

As the year went on, I realised that her memory was no longer working properly. Her conversation would go into closed loops and she would repeat things she had said only a few minutes earlier. She wanted to move back to the house permanently although she realised that she couldn't cope by herself. But any discussion about getting more help in at home was doomed to failure. She was unable to focus on detailed plans and would return to agonising about her deteriorating health and her unhappiness about living in an institution, populated by ghosts. She had known some of her fellow residents when they were all young and alert and it was distressing to see them in such a pitiful state. One of them, wandering slowly round the sitting room, had been a teenage tennis champion.

In the summer, I discovered that I could fly quite cheaply from Heathrow to Leeds and avoid the tedious drive up and down the M1. Marion met me at the airport and we did some food shopping for my weekend with Florrie. By this time she was getting more resigned to staying in the Carmel, but would still go into long plaints about how unhappy she was. She now needed regular help with dressing while we were at the house and bemoaned the state of her underwear which was indeed, threadbare and fraying at the edges. I pondered how it would be possible for me to buy her some replacements which would be acceptable, knowing how particular she was. But she was grateful for my help and told me that I couldn't have looked after her better if I'd been a daughter! I took this as a compliment, and forgiveness for having been another boy. I was also uneasily aware that she had been unable to accept her daughters-in-law as daughters. Pat had shown her great kindness since Manny's death, but had felt she had never been loved as a daughter. My brothers and their wives were often angry with our mother and, to my mind, lacking in patience. I think I was better able to just listen to her tirades, which were sometimes reproachful (no one loves her) rather than trying to correct her version of events. Perhaps I was better at detaching myself emotionally when the complaints began? On the other hand, I suspect that, as the 'baby' of the family, less was expected of me and I was given an easier time.

Then the house was burgled. Florrie's small collection of silver, on display in a cabinet in the rear lounge was all taken, but mercifully the house wasn't trashed. In the front room everything was intact including the brass knick-knacks on the mantelpiece and the framed photographs. Later we heard that the police had recovered the silver and it was returned to the cabinet, only to be stolen a second time and never seen again. This time, the burglars also smashed a window and took her television. It seemed that our house, left unguarded and unoccupied except during my weekend visits, was under recurrent attack. How long could it last? Michael and Kenneth agreed that it would have to be sold. I could see their logic but I was dismayed at the idea of not being able to take Florrie back any more, and not to be able to go there myself. I began to realise how important the house was to me. I briefly thought about buying it myself, to keep it in the family. But this was not really on. We couldn't afford it and there would be few opportunities to use it unless we moved to Leeds which Mary didn't want, and even I didn't want to do. Our life was in London. And so the house was put up for sale. Did Florrie consent? I suppose she must have done, although I kept out of these discussions and left the difficult and unwelcome task to my elder brothers. I did meet the prospective buyers, a nice young couple with a toddler. At least, I thought, my old house would be in good hands. Another little boy could sleep in my room and venture through the gate in the back garden into the field beyond. But Florrie was not so sanguine. When she heard that the sale was going through she kept repeating, how did I lose my home? Then, before the new owners could move in, the burglars attacked a third time and we heard that the house was 'in a terrible mess' with drawers emptied and clothes and papers scattered everywhere. I felt personally violated and grieved for the indignity and suffering of my old home. In fact, when Michael and I went to clear it up, it wasn't too bad.

A few weeks later, the three sons and their wives went round the house removing any articles of value or sentimental attachment before the professional house clearers did their work. When we went to see her in her room at the Carmel clutching the goods we had salvaged (clothes, photographs, pictures) she wept and called us all 'traitors'. We all felt hurt, but privately I thought there was some truth in the accusation and wondered if I could still stop the sale going through. When the others left, I showed her some old photographs and letters which she liked, and we parted as friends. I took the card-table round to Marion's for safekeeping.

In the New Year, I took her round in a wheel chair to say goodbye to the house. We couldn't go in any more as the new owners had taken possession, but we gazed at the outside for a while. She asked me to wheel her down the side to the top of the garden steps, from where we could see the view that she liked to look at through the kitchen windows. 'Not a bad house to live in for 55 years' was her final, understated verdict. She said she didn't want to stay in Leeds, with 'no family and no home'. She talked about walking out of the Carmel and going back home. Did she realise this was now physically impossible for her? It must have been like one of those dreams in which you try to escape from a trapped situation but your legs won't move. Since I had been unable to keep the house, my next plan was to get her to come to London so that she would be able to see two of her sons and some of her grandchildren. I baulked at the idea of having her to stay in our house, reasoning that it was too small, she couldn't manage the steps, and she needed a lot of personal care. Perhaps a daughter would have done it, got the house adapted or moved to somewhere bigger. But many daughters are not so selfless with their mothers and end up putting them in a Home, rather than taking them home. I shall stop making excuses and just describe what happened. We booked her into a care home not far away from where we live, for a short stay, with the possibility of a longer one. She hated it from the beginning, and was quite angry. She demanded to be taken straight back to the Carmel. So I drove her back after only 48 hours (half of the time spent in our house). Slightly to my surprise, the staff greeted her with open arms and she seemed as pleased to be back as if it had really been her home.

We had a nice mother-and-son weekend in Leeds that August. The weather was good, so Marion and I took Florrie to the local flower show in her wheelchair. She took a lively interest in all the flowers, fruits and comical giant vegetables. She admired the handicrafts. She even had an ice cream. Best of all, we met Barry Brown, Michael's best friend from his student days, who greeted her enthusiastically. It was nice to see her smiling and animated after all the distress of the past year. We had tea at Marion's house; I took her 'home' and then drove back to London. I wished I could do more to fix things for her. To get her new clothes and a new watch (hers had stopped) and mend the television set in her room and stop this deterioration of all her possessions along with her health. Being 200 miles away made everything more difficult. I did buy her a new watch with which she was very pleased, and after Christmas, (which she spent in Carmel, declining our invitation to stay) I sent her a new brassiere! At my next visit I managed to persuade her into it. It seemed a little tight but she liked to feel supported and held together.

Then Uncle Benny died from a heart attack. Florrie had been told of his death but had to keep asking us for confirmation that it was Benny and not someone else who had 'gone'. For some reason, I said to her, you're getting a bit low on brothers. She looked a bit startled and then with a sort of half smile, said, how many have I got left? I don't think she could really take it in. Her one remaining brother, Abe, died a few weeks later, released at last from his miserable post-stroke existence, unable to walk, talk, eat or drink. A whole generation had fallen.

I continued visiting every three weeks. Now that the house had gone I had to stay in a hotel. I still managed to take Florrie out for a drive or to tea with Marion. Her memory continued to deteriorate and her conversation to circulate in closed loops but she was always pleased to see me.

On 1 May 1997, Tony Blair won a landslide victory in the general election and the era of New Labour government began. I dropped in to see Florrie on my way to a conference. She had had an episode of bowel incontinence and it was difficult to summon any help. I managed to clean her up myself and find her some new pants. It was pitiful to see her getting more and more helpless. In the summer, she was admitted to hospital after a fall and Mary and I visited her there. She was asleep when we arrived but then woke up and said, I'll be lonely again when you've gone. Take me with you! It was impossible to explain why we couldn't or wouldn't do this and her repeated cries of 'take me with you' were heart-rending. We escaped, as one does from the bedrooms of old people trapped by their incapacity, simply by walking away. She was moved back to Carmel two days later.

But soon the managers felt that she was too infirm to stay at Carmel and needed more nursing care. She was moved to the main Home for the Aged. It was sunny when Mary and I visited so we all sat in the garden. Florrie was quiet and seemed to have retreated into herself. But when we got up to go inside she pointed out that I had left my jacket on the back of my chair. She was still watching out for me. Back in the lounge, with the residents sitting in their high backed chairs, the television showed continuous pictures of Princess Diana who had died in a car crash the previous day. The residents said nothing, though who knows what they were feeling.

In December 1997, Florrie developed a respiratory infection and suffered a mild stroke. She was admitted to another hospital. On her 96th birthday (21 January) she was still there, having a prolonged convalescence. When I telephoned, the nurse said she was much better apart from a tendency to shout for no obvious reason. I flew to Leeds the following weekend and found her in 'The Quiet Room' which was decorated and furnished in 1940s style to make the old people feel at home and perhaps to jog their memories. Although it was supposed to be quiet in there, I could hear Florrie's voice from down the corridor. Fortunately she was the only patient there. She was shouting in a hoarse voice, at regular intervals, a single syllable that sounded like 'LOR!' I said hello and she smiled and seemed to recognise me. When I asked if she was OK, she said 'Yes' in her normal voice. Then the shouts resumed. It looked as though she had suffered cognitive damage as a result of the stroke. I came back on Sunday morning and met Michael and Pat at the hospital. Florrie seemed brighter and more like her self. She noticed that I was wearing a new jacket and that I had a bandage on my finger where I had trapped it in the car door. When left alone she continued to do her shouts and we realised that she was actually shouting the word LOVE! I wondered if this was her final message to the world. That love is all you need, or all that remains of us, or something like that. Later on, I asked a consultant physician in Care of the Elderly whether this was possible. He said that it was quite common for elderly people with brain damage to repeat a single word; the word was produced entirely at random, was not a communication and had no meaning whatsoever. I was not convinced.

When I saw her again in the spring she was back in the Home for the Elderly, but this time in a large ward on the upper floor for patients who were bed-bound and likely to disturb others. She seemed smaller and frailer than before and at first I only just recognised her. By the window, another ancient one sat facing the wall, reciting an Alzheimer litany which sounded like the patter of a deranged musical hall compere: And now, we present to you, the ladies of the universe. We'll be back next week, but now, tonight, we're going home. Yes, tonight, ladies and gentlemen, we're taking her home.

But I can't, I'm not well enough. protested Florrie from her corner.

I hurried to reassure her. Then she settled down and went back to her own refrain of 'Love – love – love'.

The only sense I got out of her after that was when she gazed at me and said: You look like my brother Harry.

Then along came Derek, bearded, genial, auxiliary nurse who fed her carefully with a spoon. When I told him she had studied to be a doctor but only for year, he paused and said, Florence, why did you give up medicine?

Too difficult, she replied.

I said goodbye and left, feeling that she was in good hands.

After that, although I continued to make the journey by plane, train or car, it was difficult to have any kind of conversation with her. She couldn't walk, could hardly talk, except to call out 'Love!' And even that was no longer loud enough to disturb anyone.

On one occasion she was a bit tetchy with me at first. She said, Can I trust you? What am I doing here? When can we go? But then she calmed down and asked about the children. After that, she just slept and I held her hand. She smiled and waved when I left. I felt I should have stayed and held her hand all day, but I didn't.

In December, Auntie Tess died. Now, of those four Rostov siblings and their wives only Florrie and Benny's wife Ada remained. I saw Florrie but I'm not sure that she recognised me specifically.

It can't be helped, she said at one point. And then: It's my fault.

I saw her for the last time a few weeks later. She looked small and fragile but quite well apart from some obvious left-sided facial weakness. I think she knew me this time but she didn't say much. Most of the time she just repeated 'love' very softly. For a while, a distressed and anguished expression came over face. And then, she relaxed again. I gave her a couple of hugs and thanked her for being my Mum. I don't know if she understood. It felt like Goodbye. A week later I was woken at 6.30 a.m. to be told that she had 'faded away' in the night. We all travelled to Leeds the next day, for her funeral. The remaining Rostovs and a few Levinskys gathered at the Old Age Home and went off once again, in a cortège of cars, to that strange cemetery. The ceremony and the rather brutal burial were similar to Manny's. Except that beside the gaping oblong of raw clay, there was a newish white gravestone. My father's. I felt that we should have another gathering to celebrate her life properly, but we never did. As I stood at the graveside, I thought: she was my Mum and she did her best. She was loving. Sometimes she was brave, though often she was afraid. She suffered all that depression and anxiety and those pointless compulsive behaviours. She was protected and cherished by my father, although at times she must have driven him to the brink of despair. They both struggled. And now they lie side by side. He has been there for 25 years. Soon she will have a stone as well; there will be a pair of stones. Cold in the earth and the deep snow piled above thee, as Emily says. I felt a ridiculous sense of comfort that they were resting together.

Epilogue

I wonder if, in those last few days of drifting in and out and slowly fading away, Florrie thought about or recollected her long life. Did it appear before her inward gaze as a series of scenes, visions or hallucinations? Or was it more like a dream? I like to think that she had an opportunity to review at least some of the many events and encounters, the sense impressions and the emotions that I have attempted to describe, at first from her point of view and later from mine. I imagine that it would have been chronologically in reverse order, in the manner used by some biographical filmmakers as their stories come to an end. She would see herself, first of all, lying helpless in her bed in the high dependency ward. Then, the dream begins. She puts aside the bedcovers and rises to her feet. Her legs are strong again. She is fully dressed and walking easily down the Harrogate Road towards the house she loves.

Manny is there, sitting by the window in the dining room reading the paper. She makes supper for them both in the kitchen. Her friends arrive to play bridge. They are all in young middle age pleased to see her and full of life. The scene dissolves and her brother Harry is sitting in his usual armchair, sipping his whisky and telling one of his stories. John is listening, entranced, He is about 12. The doorbell rings and her grandchildren arrive with their parents. She loves to watch the children playing and talk to them about their lives. Now she is on holiday; a swift montage of scenes shows her in Torquay and Falmouth with Manny; then in Paris, and Lugano, with Manny and John. This scene is interrupted by the harsh wail of an air raid siren and the blue waters of Lake Lugano vanish. She is in the middle of the evacuation crowd, saying goodbye to Michael and Kenneth. Then they are arriving at the new house for the first time and the boys are rushing delightedly into the field, followed by Manny while she watches them through the wide kitchen window.

Now she is on the beach at Bridlington surrounded by her whole family: her parents in deckchairs, the boys playing cricket, Benny taking his photographs. The beach disappears and they are sitting round the table at her parents' house having a traditional lunch and listening to Tommy Handley on the radio. The laughter and applause fade away to be replaced by the calm voice of Dr Eder asking her about her latest dream as she lies on his couch, twisting a handkerchief in her hands. Now she is sitting on little Michael's bed, willing him not to die as he chokes and wheezes. Manny and Dr Samuel appear at the door and that scene fades to her wedding day in her bridal dress with her handsome husband beside her. Now she is talking and laughing with her university friends. The war has just ended and they say a new world is beginning. Jimmy Barclay appears and gives her the little gold heart. He tells her he has been killed in the war and won't be coming back. But Florrie is suddenly back in her parents' home, looking after her mischievous little brothers. She runs down the street, shouting Harry, where are you, but he is nowhere to be seen. Suddenly he pops out from behind a corner. She takes his hand and leads him back into the house where her mother and father are waiting for them, smiling. She climbs onto her father's knee, and strokes his whiskers. Another family photograph is to be taken with all her brothers, cousins, uncles and aunts posed outside the front of the house in Brunswick Place. She is the little girl in the front row with a serious expression and a white ribbon in her hair.